Strategic Acquisition: A Smarter Way to Grow A Business

2nd edition

David Annis and Gary Schine

CONTENTS

Introduction

It's quite simple— the way to expand your business is through hard work. Keep your customers happy and market aggressively. In the end it comes down to old-fashioned sales and marketing, and plenty of hard work. This simple formula is what most consultants, professors, and businessmen will insist is the way to grow your business. You'll hear a lot of truisms like "There are no shortcuts to success."

We're certainly not about to claim that hard work isn't a key ingredient of success in growing a business. However, contrary to the traditional wisdom, there is a shortcut to growth. Growth through acquisition, too often considered the exclusive domain of the largest companies, is also quite appropriate for small and midsize companies looking to achieve rapid expansion.

Growth through acquisition is a quicker, cheaper, and far less risky proposition than the tried and true methods of expanded marketing and sales efforts. Furthermore, acquisition offers a myriad of other advantages such as easier financing and instant economies of scale. The competitive advantages are also formidable, ranging from catching one's competition off guard, to instant market penetration even in areas where you may currently be weak, to the elimination of a competitor through its acquisition.

Synergistic acquisition is not limited to buying direct competitors. We will also detail how small and mid-size companies can efficiently grow by buying related or complimentary companies. It is quite common for a company to buy another to take better advantage of each other's distribution channels. For example, a candy manufacturer with several retail outlets might purchase a specialty food mail order (or e-commerce) company. The buying company could then use the mail order company's distribution channels to sell its candy. If it were a really good fit, it could also offer some of the mail order firm's products through its retail outlets.

Another fairly common type of acquisition involves the purchase of a company in the same industry but in a different geographic area. Internet Service Provider companies, for example, often buy ISP's in other regions. Cost center elements like customer service and billing can be centralized to gain economies of scale by spreading the costs of billing and service systems over the dramatically increased volume of business.

Few major companies have grown to where they are today without acquiring at least a few companies along the way. Many of the Fortune 500 companies achieved membership in that exclusive club by relying quite extensively on external growth strategies. This history of growth via acquisition is particularly true in rapidly changing industries such as telecommunications and high technology. Successful companies in less volatile industries like groceries, home construction products, and certainly banking also often rely on acquisition to achieve growth, market share, economies of scale, and marketing clout.

The benefits of growth through acquisition are hardly limited to marketing. It is typically easier to finance growth via acquisition than via more traditional routes of expansion. As we'll demonstrate, lenders and investors are more impressed by historical financial statements than with projections based business plans, no matter how positive the projections may be. Furthermore, a whole otherwise non-existent form of financing is available through the common practice of seller financing. That is, business buyers typically pay some of the sales price over a period of several years at interest rates below those of bank lending rates.

The catalyst driving many business acquisitions involves synergies. When companies are merged together, the whole is often greater than the sum of its parts. Synergies involving marketing and economies of scale, as stated earlier, are clear benefits. Also, there are typically opportunities involving production, volume discounts in purchasing, and reduced overhead expenses as a percentage of sales.

Conventional Wisdom & Acquisition Wisdom

Build Customer Loyalty and Sell Aggressively, and Growth Will Follow

The conventional wisdom, which this book will challenge, is based on time-honored principles. As with many time-honored principles, they have been subject to less and less consideration over time, so eventually their wisdom stops being questioned and they are accepted without examination.

For example, it's almost an axiom that to grow, it is essential to gain trust and customer loyalty. Trust and loyalty are achieved by consistently doing a superior job and gaining a top-notch reputation. Now, a good job and a top-notch reputation are certainly admirable characteristics and business advantages. However, they are not always the most essential ingredients to growth. Even companies with less-than-stellar reputations and fickle customers can and do grow through acquisition. We're not saying to discount a well-developed reputation. We are saying that this is only one route to growth, and while it may offer a sense of control, it is not necessarily the least risky or the fastest way to achieve success.

Another unchallenged principle is that business success and growth go only to the most aggressive business people. Aggressiveness is a valuable trait, but it is manifest in a number of ways. Usually when advisors coach business owners to be more aggressive they mean aggressiveness in terms of sales efforts. "Knock on more doors, don't take no for an answer, do what you must to get that sale; that's how you'll grow." Business is a broad enough field that success can come from a number of directions and can come to people with varying personalities. Being a "don't take no for an answer" sales person can be helpful, but it is not necessarily the only or even the most efficient mode of growing a business. Acquisition may well be a more efficient means of growth than a super charged sales effort.

You Need to Take Big Risks to Grow

Another truism we challenge is that small business owners must take big risks if they intend to grow. The conventional wisdom says, "The more rapidly you want to grow, the bigger the risks you must take." Every entrepreneur understands that risk is a part of business. However, that doesn't mean huge risks are necessary on a regular basis and it doesn't mean there is anything wrong with minimizing risk to the extent possible. A lot of growth can indeed come from taking risks in the hope of a sizable return. A lot of growth can also come from the lower risk route of acquisition.

We can't argue that acquisition is without risk. We can argue that the risks are not only smaller but are also far easier to anticipate and quantify than are the more traditional risks associated with growth. For one thing, the expenses of an acquisition can be projected with reasonable accuracy. The expenses associated with more traditional growth strategies are far less predictable when measured against a clear objective. Suppose you're running a $10 million company and want to grow by 50%. Suppose there is a $5 million company for sale for $2 million. Your 50% growth will cost $2 million. Under this scenario, your likelihood of achieving your 50% growth goal is very near 100%.

Suppose you instead decided on a more traditional method of achieving 50% growth such as increased promotion or increased sales effort. How much would it cost? How long would it take? How likely is it that the projected number of dollars spent would achieve the stated growth goal?

An acquisition strategy may well be cheaper, is probably quicker, and is certainly less risky in terms of meeting the stated objective at the anticipated cost.

Don't Grow Too Fast

Rapid growth comes with some dangers. Some otherwise successful companies have actually gone under due to rapid growth. While growth is enviable, it is by nature problematic. Spur of the moment management decisions must be made regularly and without benefit of adequate supporting information. Money and resources must be expended in advance of projected increased revenues, or one runs the risk of not being equipped to adequately deal with the new business efficiently, thereby alienating customers.

For example, in a modest growth environment, existing employees can generally accommodate the modest increases in responsibilities and volume of work. When they become stretched, orderly hiring can begin. Likewise, when facilities become cramped, you can start seeking new space to rent or buy. However, when growth is taking place at, say, 45% a year, making the decisions of when to hire, when to buy new capital equipment, and when to expand facilities become significantly more complex. Expending a lot of money and other resources too early can be very wasteful. But making the expenditures too late can be disastrous in that all sorts of problems will occur in trying to please the new customers that your marketing efforts (and dollars) worked so hard to secure.

Contrast the seat-of-the-pants decision and plan making of this kind of expansion with an acquisition. First, you know within a small margin of error what your expanded volume will be because you're buying a defined customer base with a history and possibly even contracts that specify future delivery schedules. You can look at the purchase history of the customers that you are acquiring, and examine it in detail, including looking at how volatile sales volume has been. That gives you a far better picture of future sales than guessing at future sales that are based on unknowns such as opening new locations, increased advertising, or hiring new salespeople.

Second, systems and procedures will be in place to handle the increased sales. The selling company has the facilities, procedures, and even the employees in place to deal with the new business smoothly and without the need for quick decisions and interventions. After all, though it's new business to you, it's business they've been doing for some time. You may elect to make changes in procedures, but you won't need to do so immediately, and you probably won't want to do so until you have watched and analyzed the systems that you acquired as part of the company you purchased.

An expansion of any type comes with challenges, sometimes wrenching challenges as a business enters uncharted territory. An acquisition may have a few surprises and challenges, but they are likely to be controllable, far more controllable than the uncharted territory of traditional rapid expansion. Spur of the moment decisions without adequate information will be the exception, not the rule. Conventional wisdom is that growth should be kept in the 5% to 20% per year range in most industries. If you expand much more than that the danger increases exponentially. "Control your growth; take the time necessary to digest the new business (and new challenges) that come from your growth efforts. Consider the fact that new customers you've gained, particularly if you've stolen them from a competitor, are fickle customers and need to receive special attention and TLC to retain their loyalty. The longer a customer has been a customer of yours, the less likely he is to be wooed away by a competitor." This advice is the kind that a small business owner is likely to hear.

Even if a confident entrepreneur wants to ignore the advice, he's likely to hit a brick wall in financing his ambitious expansion. Bankers, not known for challenging convention, will take a dim view of business plans projecting quick growth of, say. 60% to 80% or more. They, too, will scold you about being unrealistic and not understanding the dangers of excessively rapid growth. Although you may disagree with the conventional views of bankers who believes that your projected growth is too ambitious and risky, you are unlikely to convince any banker to provide financing based on extremely aggressive growth projections.

In this type of aggressive growth scenario, acquisition wins hands down. Companies regularly acquire their way to 50%, 100%, and even higher growth rates overnight through acquisitions. The warnings about overly rapid growth just don't apply because the systems, personnel, and equipment handling the growth are in place in the form of the business you just bought. Sure, they may need some tweaking and changing to fit in with your own procedures, but chances are they are serviceable for a period of time, and that the adjustment will be relatively easy to achieve, at least relative to rapid growth by more traditional methods.

As for financing, the argument gets even more compelling. Not only do bankers accept growth through acquisition, but even prefer it to even modest traditional growth. Bankers are taught to make projections based on past financial performance as demonstrated through historic financial statements. They pay lip service to business plans, but they want to see tangibles, in terms of assets that they can take away from you if necessary, and in terms of past performance from which they can draw inferences regarding cash flow. When you buy a company, you can show them what they want to see in their own language— the financial statements of the selling company.

Consider this scenario:

Banker: "Well, Mr. Owner, just what are you basing your ambitious projections of a $1,000,000 sales increase upon?"

You: "Well, Mr. Banker, I'm basing it on the sales of the company we are buying, which are about $1,000,000. Here are the company's financial statements for the past three years. Notice the annual cash flow of $200,000, which will come in very handy for repaying the loan."

If this isn't advantage enough, consider that you may not even need the banker, because sellers often will provide some of the cash needed to buy their company through owner financing. That's right, owners will often lend you much of the money to buy their business, accept lower interest rates, and may accept the assets of the business you're buying as sole security! Finally, consider the argument about new customers being fickle customers. When you buy a company, what you're largely buying is an established customer base. In many industries, a higher price is paid for customers that have been customers of that business for a longer time. Your new customers are not new customers. Sure, they're new to you, but they'll keep doing business with the same company that they've been doing business with for years. The only difference: you'll now own that company.

Only Large Companies Need Apply

It's no secret that larger, publicly traded companies buy other companies regularly. Though it tends to be called a "merger and acquisition," it's the same thing with a fancier name.

At least several times a month, the business pages carry a headline like "Amazon.com is buying Zappos.com" or "Microsoft is buying yet another software company."

Somehow, owners of smaller businesses assume that mergers and acquisitions is a Wall Street game that is not appropriate for small businesses to play. Some of the mechanics are different. For example, there can be no hostile takeovers of privately held companies and your acquisition probably won't be reported on CNBC. But the rationale is just as compelling and the benefits are at least as real for a small privately held company as for a large publicly held firm.

Synergies and Economies of Scale

The benefits realized in a strategic acquisition are largely a result of synergies and economies of scale. In a well-executed acquisition, the acquiring company can take advantage of synergies. That is, the two companies together will be stronger and more profitable than either company was previously.

Synergy is roughly defined as two or more things together being better or more effective than the sum of their parts. As it's used here, it means two or more companies merging such that the combined resources of the merged unit have more than the sum of the value they had individually.

For example, suppose XYZ Engineering Company has very skilled sales and marketing people. Through their marketing abilities, they have a number of contracts for sophisticated engineering projects. However, their engineering staff leaves something to be desired. The engineers are inexperienced and are not well equipped to handle the contracts that XYZ sales personnel are able to secure.

ABC Engineering Company has opposite strengths and weaknesses. This firm is made up of top flight engineers. However, ABC does not have strong marketing abilities, so it holds few contracts despite its engineering superiority to XYZ. The obvious solution is to merge ABC and XYZ into one company. XYZ's marketing staff could secure contracts, while ABC's engineers could complete the jobs.

While this example is simplistic, it demonstrates a powerful business concept that is being exercised all the time by companies of all sizes. Some of this nation's most successful firms owe their success largely to external growth strategies that capitalize on the synergistic logic.

As we've discussed, conventional wisdom maintains that growth comes through delivering quality products and services and effectively marketing those products and services. While this conventional method is one effective means to growth, it is not the only one. Another way to add customers, leads, production capabilities, and other intangible assets is to buy them.

Economies of Scale

Production economies of scale are obvious in an acquisition. Undeniable benefits of scale will be realized when a production facility is suddenly operating at, say, 85% of capacity rather than 50%. However, the economies of scale don't end with production. They also come into play in marketing, administration, professional expertise, purchasing, and other areas.

Most successful acquisitions are based largely on the concepts of synergies and economies of scale. Marketing synergies and production synergies drive many acquisitions. However, synergistic advantages can also result from strategically combining expertise, complimentary products, and several types of economies of scale. Add the advantages that acquisition is easier to finance and decidedly quicker and less risky to implement than more traditional growth strategies, and you have a powerful alternative route to rapid expansion. This lower-risk shortcut to growth is every bit as appropriate to smaller businesses as to larger ones.

Marketing Logic

The marketing advantages alone can more than justify many acquisitions. Some of the advantages detailed below dwarf the incremental improvements that more familiar marketing methods will bring. What's more, a growth through acquisition strategy will probably be cheaper and almost certainly less risky than the typical uphill marketing campaign will be.

Acquiring Saves Marketing Dollars and Avoids Risk

Some novice entrepreneurs, and all too many new MBAs, think that they can develop marketing campaigns that are so good that sales will increase by huge percentages and take profits on a similar journey up the growth chart. While such campaigns are possible, in a competitive landscape where competitors respond by countering with their own new marketing and pricing strategies, it is difficult to sustain extremely rapid growth through marketing efforts alone. Those of us who have been around marketing for a while know that more typically, promotion results in incremental increases in sales and profits. Expecting a single ad or single ad campaign to quickly double sales is not realistic, at least not at an affordable cost. A more reasonable standard for most promotion is the return it garners beyond its cost. When a business owner spends money on advertising and as a result adds enough sales to covers his advertising and other variable costs, along with a reasonable profit margin, the owner is usually satisfied with the result.

Most of us who have been around marketing for a while also understand its inherent risks, particularly when varying from the tried and true methods. For example, let's say ABC Digital is a computer repair service that has been in business for six years. For promotion, ABC relies solely on direct mail campaigns that routinely yield a 2% response with a 50% conversion to sales rate. Perhaps the ultimate cost of this marketing is $120 per new client recruited. Let's suppose this company wants to expand more quickly than its single method marketing will allow. There are, of course, a myriad of promotional possibilities: newspaper advertising, radio, TV, Internet, direct sales, etc. However, as none of those have been used or even tested, they all involve significant risk. They may succeed in that that they may bring in clients at a cost of, say, $90 per customer—$30 less per customer than the tried and true method. They may also bring disappointing results in that the cost will end up being $150 per customer or even may result in a net loss if the new revenues can't cover advertising and incremental expenses.

Let's look at another possibility for expansion for this fictitious computer repair business. Let's say the owner has built the business to about $1,000,000 in revenues, but has decided he's gone as far as he can go with direct mail as his primary growth vehicle. His goal is ambitious—a 25% increase over the next year. He understands that to achieve his objectives he'll have to increase his advertising expense significantly on a total expenditure basis, and probably on a per client gained basis as well. He's talked to all the advertising salesmen he wants to talk to and heard each sales pitch about how advertising is an investment and how it takes many repetitions before an ad really pays for itself. They all stop short of anything approaching a promise and all look at him like he has two heads when he tries to negotiate a deal involving payment based on sales from the ad. Now, of course, there are internet-based pay-per-click advertisements and affiliate programs, but for a computer repair company that is looking to build long term, complex relationships with clients, sales seldom happen exclusively on a website. Even for a web based retailer, there is a point of diminishing returns in advertising expenditures.

While he's pondering his decision he learns that a small competitor of his, called XYZ Technologies, may be interested in selling his business. ABC and XYZ compete for the same types of customers—small businesses with two to ten computers at a single facility. He learns that he can buy this business for $250,000. XYZ claims a customer base of about 2,200 customers and gross sales of $350,000, which translates to sales of about $160 per customer per year. At this price, the acquisition would cost about $114 per customer. This rate is competitive with his direct mail response rate, far less risky than any of the untried promotional possibilities, and he would gain those new customers right away; there would be no ramp-up time.

He learns that while the price of $250,000 can't be negotiated any further, the terms may be flexible. Perhaps the owner would accept some of the payment over time or on a contingency basis (a partial credit for customer attrition), reducing the risk and initial cash outlay even further. We'll get into financing possibilities and advantages in a later chapter. For now, let's focus on the marketing advantages of this simplified but far from unreasonable scenario as summarized in the following chart.

Increase Promotion	Acquire Business
Promotional costs with uncertain results	Customers already exist; only risk is some attrition of customer base
25% growth projected	35% increase (minus attrition estimated at 5% to 7%)
Time frame: about a year	Time frame: immediately upon closing the sale
Costs paid as incurred (mostly advertising)	Some costs paid on delivery of actual customer base; some deferred based on negotiations with seller

Acquiring a Channel

A common marketing goal of acquisition is the merging and sharing of distribution channels. A distribution channel, or more to the point a customer base, typically takes years of hard work to develop. However, acquisition can be a very effective shortcut. For example:

A distributor of outdoor furniture, which we'll call Yard and Patio Furniture Co., had been selling its products to garden and patio retailers for over 15 years. The company's owner wanted to expand. He was familiar with the tried and true methods of growing a business; he had been using them for 15 years. In the past he had grown by hiring sales people to knock on doors, advertising by direct mail, and advertising by telemarketing. All of the methods worked to some degree, and all involved risking time and money.

With our help, the owner looked at the alternative possibility of growth through acquisition. Together we set the following acquisition goals for the company:

a) Add a new synergistically appropriate product line(s) that could be sold to Yard and Patio's current customer base.

b) Add a new customer base for Yard and Patio's line of outdoor furniture.

c) Increase Yard and Patio's sales and profits, while limiting the corresponding increase in overhead.

After looking for a period of six months, this firm found and bought a company that imports specialized planters and wholesales them to garden and patio shops. Now, Yard and Patio can sell its furniture to the acquired company's customers, and sell the acquired company's planters to its own furniture customers. The two companies were geographically far enough apart that there was very little overlap in customers.

In another example, a large company owned a regional west coast manufacturing firm that made plumbing fixtures for mobile homes. It purchased a Midwestern manufacturer of mobile home heating devices. Both companies sold to the same industry, mobile home manufacturers, but in different geographic regions. The goals here were to instantly gain a Midwestern distribution channel for the west coast company and a west coast channel for the Midwest firm. Now, this firm is selling plumbing and heating devices in both the West and Midwest by exploiting its pre-existing and its acquired distribution channels. The company is trying to find and purchase similar firms in other regions to expand further, using the same synergistic strategy.

In both of these instances, developing new customers by relying on the traditional bag of tricks of sales and marketing would have been a far more cumbersome, expensive, and time consuming undertaking than was the path chosen. In fact, in the case of the mobile home component example, the acquired company nearly doubled its volume overnight through the acquisition. The buying company has gone from a 300 million dollar firm ten years ago to a 1.2 billion dollar firm today, primarily through its synergistic external growth strategy.

This type of acquisition of a channel is another potential advantage of buying a company. Gaining resellers is clearly one of the major challenges facing wholesalers. Once retailers are secured as customers, they tend to remain as customers. It is far easier for a wholesaler already supplying a reseller to introduce new items than it is for a new wholesaler to break in with a reseller no matter how good his products, services, or prices may be. Many large and even some small bookstores, for example, have a policy of refusing to consider books from wholesalers or publishers who aren't already selling to them. However, when existing publishers come out with a new title, as they do on a regular basis, it is an easy sell to get that title on the bookstore shelf, at least on a test basis.

Using the bookstore example, consider a small publisher with great new books but no secured resellers. If he tries to get bookstores to even test his great titles, he is likely to be disappointed. However, if he acquires a company already on the vendor list of a number of stores, his selling job is far easier.

Add Value to Existing Channel

Currently, we are working with an electronic connector manufacturer that sells to companies that assemble electronic devices. This company is seeking to acquire a company that manufactures related products such as electronic cables or power devices. The logic here is that the same customers who are already regularly purchasing connectors also purchase electronic cables, power supplies, etc. just as regularly. If this company is successful in finding a manufacturer of complimentary products, it can then add those products to its own connector offerings that are sold to its customer base. They will sell its connectors through the acquired company's reseller channels as well.

It is fair to say that many businesses that have gone through the effort of setting up a stable of resellers, distribution channels, are under-utilizing those channels. A company selling only its current products through those channels and letting others reap the benefits of complimentary product sales is selling itself short. An acquisition is a viable remedy to this shortfall.

Promotion Synergies & Economies

There aren't too many services that better demonstrate the concept of economies of scale then the printing industry. Print 1,000 brochures and it may cost $200, or 20 cents per piece. Print 2,000 and it may cost $250, or 8 cents each piece, 60% less on a per piece basis. The more you print, the cheaper it is on a unit cost basis. Even in the high-tech 21st century, printing is still an integral component of marketing campaigns, so saving on printing costs alone can contribute to bottom line profitability. The same kinds of saving, though perhaps less dramatic than the printing example, can also be realized in space advertising, media advertising, or any other service where eager salesmen will offer better prices for higher volume purchases.

The economies don't end with quantity discounts, though. Consider the cost of creating a product catalog or a web site with online ordering. In either case, doubling the number of products offered will not come close to doubling your costs. It may increase costs by, say, 20%. Just like in the printing example, this web catalog example drastically lowers the per item cost. Also, it arguably makes for a stronger catalog or web site in that more products offered can lead to a synergistic effect in purchasing, as your catalog becomes more of a one-stop-shopping vehicle.

Increase Market Share

Years ago a local businessman approached us because he wanted to buy a business for his daughter. I told him about a package and mailing storefront business for sale. He thought about it and said, "Well, if you can find two or three more for sale in the same area, I might be interested, but I don't want to buy just this one." His logic: a small storefront location would have a very hard time competing with the heavyweight competition from franchises like *Mailboxes Etc.* However, with a few locations in the same area where brand identification could be established and economies of scale could be achieved, his daughter would have a chance to compete on closer to equal footing. She also would be able to concentrate her competitive efforts on the franchises and not have to worry about the independents in the area.

Market share equals market clout. By acquiring a company in your own industry. you can gain that market share immediately and the market influence that comes with it. A company with a formidable market share can more confidently make pricing and other business decisions rather than merely respond to what others are doing. For example, a large long distance carrier can risk increasing its prices without losing too many customers, even if the increase would mean other smaller companies might provide long distance services cheaper in some localities. In all likelihood, if a dominant printing company in a community raised their prices, smaller printers would soon follow their lead and raise prices as well. Smaller companies don't enjoy the economies of scale of the large printer. Paradoxically, they would probably need the increase more than the much larger company would, in order to earn a profit given the less favorable cost structures. However, the small printer would be taking a huge risk if it raises its prices before the larger printer does.

The same logic can work in niche marketplaces. Supermarket pricing of vegetables will have influence on how local farm stands set their prices, though the supermarket will probably not be too influenced by the farm stand prices.

Finally, in the case of an expanding market, the larger your market share, the more your sales are carried along with the increases. As the entire market for, say, beer grows, Anheuser Busch, with its dominating market share, will be a large beneficiary. As the market for greeting cards increases, Hallmark will benefit more than smaller greeting card companies will.

One Fewer Competitor

If some of the above discussion of market share seems too theoretical for a smaller business, here's a clear and practical benefit of buying a competitor. Quite simply: after the purchase, you have one fewer competitor. Now, in a market with lots of competition, one fewer may not be that big of a deal, but consider this real situation. Years ago, one of the authors was approached by a typing and copying service in the heart of an urban college campus area. They wanted to sell their company, which was marginally profitable. It didn't take a lot of research to find a buyer. The company's only neighborhood competitor was a block away. We approached the competing company, arguing that if he bought his only competitor he would be able to increase prices, and would not have to jump through as many hoops to please his demanding clientele. After all, the threat of going down the street to his competitor would no longer mean much if he owned that competitor. He bought the argument and the company. The students may not have been too happy, but the owner of the only typing and copying service in this area was very happy.

Meeting and Exceeding Your Nut (Shrink Your Overhead Percentage)

Economies of scale typically involve one form or another of quantity buying in order to get a per unit cost advantage. For example, it may cost $500 to print 1,000 brochures, but $800 to print 3,000 brochures. Furthermore, the cost of designing the brochure won't change no matter how many you print. Another element of the economies of scale advantage to acquisition involves gaining cost efficiencies in meeting general business overhead, often called meeting your nut. Just about every business has some expenses that it must meet each month, whether the month is a sales record breaker or a sales disaster. Most businesses have excess productions capacity. That is, they can produce more product without increasing their fixed overhead. Most drug stores can fill at least a few more prescriptions without buying new pharmacy equipment or hiring more pharmacists. Most delivery services can deliver more packages without hiring new drivers and buying new trucks, etc. The necessity of efficiently meeting overhead was brought home to one of the authors early in his small business career. Just out of business school, he started a video production business. He was able to persuade a bank to lend his fledgling corporation money to buy the cameras, editing equipment, and the other expensive equipment that a video production company needs in order to operate.

As he and his partner were celebrating and admiring their state of the art setup, two frightening thoughts occurred to him. Both thoughts had been in the back of his mind for a while, but now they moved rapidly and forcefully to center stage. First, the bank would soon be expecting payment number one of a long string of monthly payments of principle and interest, whether or not the new equipment was in use and earning money. Second, that equipment was depreciating in value, again, whether or not it was making money. When he shared his logic and panic with his partner, it kind of dumped cold water on their little celebration and technological admiration session. Instead, they sat down to try to figure out how they could get some customers to pay them money so that they could in turn pay the bank, and hopefully have a few dollars leftover for themselves; all this before their equipment became antiquated and worthless.

The same issue faces just about any business that relies heavily on expensive equipment and/or expensive facilities. A factory must pay the fixed expenses on its production equipment whether or not it's in use, a hotel must pay the fixed expenses on each room whether occupied or not, and an internet service provider must pay for its equipment and facilities whether their servers are at 40%, 50%, or 80% of capacity.

The challenge of getting the maximum out of every expense dollar isn't only for businesses that rely on high priced equipment and facilities. Generally, some labor costs are the same whether employees are working or waiting for work as are associated costs, such as worker's comp insurance, health insurance, payroll preparation expenses, etc. Other expenses like rent, telephone and other utilities, some taxes, professional dues, and a host of others remain relatively constant whether you're operating near or nowhere near capacity.

Just like one of the authors had to hustle to keep his young video company as near capacity as possible, many if not most other businesses have to hustle to get paying customers to first meet overhead expenses and then earn a profit. Hustling, as it's used here, meaning to sell like crazy, is the most time-honored way to achieve this essential objective. Certainly the first and most common reaction for the businessperson frightened like he was at the prospect of piling up expenses is to "get out there and sell."

Sales efforts are important for keeping a business going; there's hardly a prudent argument to the contrary. However, it would also be prudent to concurrently look at filling excess capacity by gaining customers via the acquisition route. As shown previously in this book, companies routinely acquire companies in their own industry and dramatically increase their revenues overnight while cutting way down on their excess capacity and their overhead as a percentage of their revenues. For a company with significant excess capacity, whether it is unused video production equipment, unused office space, or under-worked employees, this kind of acquisition makes a great deal of sense. Let's look at a few examples:

Some time ago, we brokered the sale of a company engaged in the prepress business. Prepress is an essential step in the color printing process, and, as the name implies, a step that is completed before printing is started. The selling company, which had sales in the $2 million range, was bought by a much larger competitor with a facility fewer than 25 miles from the selling firm's offices. Within three months of the acquisition, the buyer sold off most of the selling company's equipment and incorporated the entire operation into its existing facility. From the buyer's perspective, what they essentially did was buy the seller's customers in order to eliminate some of their own excess capacity. The savings in office rental, labor, and equipment together with the revenues from selling off the seller's equipment more than paid for the acquisition. The elimination of a major local competitor and the economies of scale resulting from a bigger operation (by $2,000,000) also increased the bottom line.

Another example: Companies of all sizes retain payroll service companies to handle the processing of payroll for their employees. The sensitive nature of the work these service companies provide makes it particularly unappealing for their clients to change to another service, so it's difficult for one company to steal customers from a competitor. Also, overhead is more or less fixed up to certain capacity levels. For example, a company may calculate that it can handle, say, 100 more client companies without adding computers, employees, office space, etc. To achieve and enhance profitability, payroll services need to decrease overhead on a percentage of gross sales basis. For these reasons, payroll companies love to acquire their competitors.

A payroll company may be struggling to get by with gross fee receipts of about $500,000 and expenses of $450,000. However, to a larger company that acquires this company, the $500,000 in revenues may stay the same or may decrease by about 5% (due to a few lost clients in the transfer) to $475,000. However, the acquired expenses of $450,000 would decrease dramatically to perhaps $200,000 (or less). So a company earning about $50,000 for its previous owner ($500,000-$450,000) will immediately be earning $200,000 for the buying company ($475,000-200,000).

Cost efficiencies achieved by reducing overhead expenses can often more than justify an acquisition, but there is no need to stop with that efficiency. More often than not, additional benefits will accrue to an acquiring company. Any business with a sizable overhead to pay can likely benefit from a well-executed acquisition of a company in the same industry. By all means, continue your aggressive sales and marketing efforts. However, acquisition can be a nice shortcut to filling excess capacity if you can find the right match.

Increasing Company Value for a Sale or Public Offering

When larger companies are sold, they command higher multiples of earnings for a variety of reasons, including:

Transaction costs: A hypothetical buyer considering both a $10,000,000 acquisition and a $5,000,000 acquisition will spend a similar amount of time and effort, incur similar legal fees, accounting fees, etc. in both transactions. When calculating the IRR of the acquisition, the buyer will be able to support a higher multiple for the business that is twice as large.

Ability to go public: Larger companies can go public and get the benefit of publicly traded multiples. The multiples on publicly traded companies are higher in part because of the increased liquidity and transparency that publicly traded companies enjoy. Even if a company does not go public, achieving the size needed to do so will in-and-of itself increase a company's value.

Access to Capital: Larger companies enjoy easier access to capital in bond and loan markets.

Effects of Scale: Larger companies can often take advantage of market opportunities and economies of scale that smaller companies cannot. Larger companies may be able to bid larger projects, devote more to research and development, and move into new markets more easily than smaller ones.

Since larger companies enjoy higher multiples, acquisitions can be very effective as a strategy for increasing the price and providing a lucrative exit for owners. Let's say, to create an oversimplified example, that you own a company with $10,000,000 in sales and $1,000,000 in EBITDA. You add two companies that each have sales of $2.5 Million and EBITDA of $250,000. You have increased your top and bottom line by 50%, but if the multiple you paid for the smaller companies was 3, the multiple you could get for your company before the acquisition was 3.5 and the post-acquisition multiple is 4 your calculation looks like this:

Post-Acquisition Price: 4 X 1,500,000 = 6,000,000
Less cost of acquisitions: 3 X 500,000 = 1,500,000

= Total Post Acquisition proceeds: $4,500,000

That compares to a pre-acquisition sale price of $3,500,000 (3.5 X 1,000,000). By completing two acquisitions you capture the increase in multiple on your existing company and on the acquired companies. In this simple example, the total value of the combined business is $1,000,000 higher after the acquisitions are completed.

In Summary

Acquisition can be a faster, cheaper, and generally more efficient path to growth for companies of any size. The risk is smaller, and financing the growth is easier. Also, acquisition can be a very effective method of increasing a company's value for future sale or for an initial public offering (IPO). Finding the right company to acquire and completing the acquisition process, however, takes some effort and still entails taking some risk.

The rest of this book details the mechanics of planning, finding, evaluating, and executing a strategic acquisition.

I. A Quick Overview of the Business Acquisition Process

This section is an overview of the buy-sell process that is detailed in the book. Of course, every business acquisition deal is different, and no deal will follow these steps to the letter. However, most strategic acquisitions do follow most of the stages outlined here.

Decide on Your Acquisition Goals (Chapter II)

Your first step is to determine your acquisition goals. We recommend that you prioritize those goals and note which ones are absolutely essential, which are important but not essential, and which are optional.

Prepare a Target Profile (Chapter II)

It's a good idea to sketch out on paper (or computer screen) the characteristics and attributes of your ideal acquisition. These characteristics would include, for example:

- Industry (especially in terms of desired synergies and/or advantages to your company)
- Size range (gross sales)
- Earnings range
- Geographic limitations
- Customer characteristics
- Management characteristics and abilities
- Technological strengths

- Distribution channels
- Customer characteristics
- Products or product lines

Search for Acquisition Candidate(s) (Chapter III)

Finding an ideal acquisition target may be the most difficult part of the process. Your task is not only finding candidates that meet your goals, but also approaching and dealing with prospective sellers who may be more than a little apprehensive about selling their companies and even about disclosing sensitive, but essential, information to you.

Evaluate Prospects (Chapter VII)

It's important to decide early on whether a prospective selling company merits serious consideration. If it does not, then there is no point in getting involved in the time-consuming and possibly expensive process of further evaluation.

You really need to evaluate both the business itself *and* the person(s) who may be selling the business. If the company looks to be perfect, but the seller seems to be unreasonable as to expectations, it's probably not worth going further. That is, you need to make a determination as to whether the owner(s) is reasonably likely to consummate a deal. To an entrepreneur who started and grew a successful company, selling it is as much an emotional decision as it is a financial one. Would-be sellers have been known to back out later in the process, after a lot of time and money have been spent.

Assume All is True

When a package of documents is presented to you that includes legalistic warnings that it is unverified and not warranted as to accuracy, it is quite appropriate to be suspicious of that information. However, in the very early stages we advise that you assume (within reason) everything presented to you is true. We're not talking about outlandish claims of potential for future growth and profits or pie-in-the-sky projections: we're talking about documents such as financial statements. Do your valuation on this basis. Just make sure that any proposal you make will give you the right to verify that everything presented to you is true and complete, during the due diligence process, and to cancel the deal without penalty if you find material inaccuracies or inconsistencies.

Valuation (Chapter VII)

Valuation is an extremely important element in the buy-sell decision. Many books have been written about it. We will cover valuation in some detail in chapter VII.

At the earliest stage we advise that you determine whether you are in negotiating range. That is, by taking a look at the financials and performing a basic valuation, it is possible to produce a ballpark estimate of the value of the acquisition target. Better still, have a third party outsider do this preliminary valuation for you to keep emotions out of it. We also have produced web based software that is appropriate for this initial valuation step at ezvaluationpro.com. If you are in negotiating range of the price set by the seller, then move on to the next step. As a rule of thumb, we figure that if the top of the buyer's range is within 30% of the seller's asking price, we are in negotiating range. If your range is, say, $2MM to $2.5MM, and the seller won't take a dollar less than $4MM, it's probably not worth going further unless he revises his price. If, however, the buyer is asking $3MM, it is worth continuing discussions.

Obtaining Further Information

Sometimes it is necessary to get further information before making even an initial evaluation. For example, financial statements give no indication of customer concentration, which can have a significant impact on valuation. Suppose there are two companies in the same industry with identical sales and earnings. However, one has 1,000 customers and the largest customer accounts for 1% of total business. The other company has 100 customers, and one of them accounts for 20% of total business, while another accounts for 15%. The company with less customer concentration would have a significantly higher value than the latter because the risk of a sudden loss of a substantial portion of the business is smaller, despite their identical sales and earnings numbers.

Sellers, especially fence-sitter sellers, can be understandably resistant to requests for further information before any type of offer or price has been discussed. At this early stage, ask only for the information you absolutely need to make your initial evaluation. Emphasize that the data can be anonymized (i.e. refer to customers as A, B, C, instead of using actual names) if doing so is realistically possible. At the same time, make it clear that if negotiations go further, you will need more information, and any preliminary offer is subject to change based on that further information.

Non-Binding Proposal and Letter of Intent(Chapter VIII)

Once you have done your preliminary evaluation we advise that you submit a non-binding proposal or "term sheet." This document outlines the terms the buyer may offer. It is designed to determine if the buyer and seller are within deal making range. Be sure that any term sheet you issue is marked with disclaimers such as "For discussion purposes only" and/or "Not an offer to purchase." Also, if there is further information you will need before issuing a Letter of Intent (LoI), say so in the proposal.

If your proposal is well received and it looks like you're in deal-making range, it's time to submit an LoI. We think of an LoI as an agreement to work toward a firm binding agreement. It outlines the terms of the deal in a bit more detail than the initial proposal does. Be careful: an LoI is a legal document that may involve a commitment on your part. Consult your attorney before issuing an LoI.

Negotiations (Chapter IX)

Chances are the seller will not agree to your LoI without some discussion and modification. Even if he does, LoIs leave many details to be worked out, so unless your proposal is rejected, there will be discussions and negotiations before the formal acquisition document is signed.

Due Diligence (Chapter X)

Due diligence is the time for full verification. While we advise that early in the process you assume that the information presented to you is true, it is at this stage where you should assume nothing. You, or more likely your accountant and your lawyer, will demand financial and other documents and information to ensure that you are buying what you think you are buying, and that there are not significant inaccuracies or misrepresentations in the information that has been presented to you.

Purchase & Sale Agreement (Chapter XI)

The purchase and sale agreement is the formal document detailing the terms of the sale as agreed to by the parties. Loose ends from the LoI are tied up in this document.

Often, the lawyers are working on the P&S while due diligence is underway. Typically, there is a good deal of back and forth between the buyer's lawyer and seller's lawyer as the details are hammered out.

Closing

The closing is the final step in the acquisition process when papers are signed, money changes hands, and the company becomes yours. Traditionally, closings take place in a lawyer's office or conference room with all the parties sitting around a table and signing lots of documents. However, many closings now are largely done using fax and email such that the principles to the deal and their legal advisors are many miles apart.

After the Sale (Chapter XIII)

Now that you own your target company, it's time to operate it to make sure it achieves the intended goals.

Your first order of business is to keep your new company's employees and customers happy. Make especially sure you keep the former owner(s), who is probably now your employee, happy.

The rest of this book goes through the steps outlined above in detail.

II. Define Your Acquisition Goals

Before going any further, you need to define what you are looking to acquire. More to the point, you need to define what benefits you are seeking for your company and how an acquisition will achieve those benefits. While there are many possible benefits that can be achieved through acquisition, not all accrue to all businesses from any particular acquisition. A great acquisition opportunity may not be so great if it doesn't achieve your acquisition objectives.

Most of the advantages of strategic acquisition fall under the general category of synergies, as discussed throughout this book. Synergy is roughly defined as two or more things together being better or more effective than the sum of their parts. As it's used here, it means two or more companies merging such that the combined resources of the merged unit have more than the sum of the value and efficiency they had individually. Recall the example earlier in this book of two engineering firms. XYZ Engineering Company has very skilled sales and marketing people. Through their marketing abilities they have a number of contracts for sophisticated engineering projects. However, their engineering staff leaves something to be desired. The engineers are inexperienced and are not well equipped to handle the contracts that XYZ sales personnel are able to sell. ABC Engineering Company has opposite strengths and weaknesses. This firm is made up of top flight engineers. However, ABC does not have strong marketing abilities, so it holds few contracts despite its engineering superiority to XYZ. The obvious solution: merge ABC and XYZ into one company. XYZ's marketing staff could secure contracts, while ABC's engineers could complete the jobs.

While this example is somewhat idealized, it demonstrates a powerful business concept that is being exercised all the time by companies of all sizes. Some of this nation's most successful firms owe their success largely to growth through acquisition or external growth strategies.

Here are a few of the ways that companies can take advantage of synergies through acquisition:

A benefit of strategic acquisition that is as straightforward as it is valuable is that of adding customers quickly and at low cost. There are numerous examples of acquisitions where the customer base is the primary target. How many times have your received a letter from your credit card company explaining that soon XYZ Bank will be your credit card company, and all the wonderful new benefits you'll receive? Well, XYZ just purchased your account and thousands of others from ABC Bank. In all likelihood, there is a stipulation for a reduction in the price paid to adjust for accounts that are cancelled before a certain date, hence the highlighting of all the new benefits.

Some customer bases are of course more valuable than others. A key determinate is the degree to which customers are locked into their current provider, and how likely they are to remain as customers through an acquisition.

Customers who are committed by long-term contract tend to have the highest value. Even contracts that can be canceled with 30 or 60 days notice are very likely to survive an ownership transition because the likelihood of losing *negative option* customers is generally quite small. Chances are, as long as the new owner keeps delivering satisfactory products or services, customers and clients will remain through a transition.

Another type of extremely valuable customer is one who is locked into the service provider in some way. For example, we recently sold a company that produced a sensor used on airplanes sold by Boeing. The sensors added about $50,000 to the price of a 777, and took two years and millions dollars to develop and certify. The company owned the intellectual property used to create the sensors. Buyers were confident that Boeing would remain a customer after the sale.

Another example of a locked-in customer is often found in customized software. One of the authors ran a software development firm and was able to remind a customer who was considering switching vendors that doing so entailed the costs of customizing the alternate vendors software, converting data to the new vendors database structure, retraining staff, time when both vendors would be paid for support, and time for testing the new software. The customer then asked for a price to add several features they liked from the alternative they were considering to their existing software, turning a potential lost customer into a customer paying for additional development.

Distribution Channels

A natural marketing goal of acquisition is the merging and sharing of distribution channels. A distribution channel or a customer base typically takes years of hard work to develop. However, acquisition can be a very effective shortcut, as is demonstrated in the examples below:

Recall the example of the distributor of outdoor furniture, called Yard and Patio Furniture Co.that had been selling its products to garden and patio retailers. It acquired a company that imports specialized planters and wholesales them to garden and patio shops. Now Yard and Patio Furniture sells its furniture to the selling company's customers, and sells the selling company's planters to its own furniture customers.

In another example we used before, a large company owned a regional West Coast manufacturing firm that made plumbing fixtures for mobile homes. It purchased a Midwestern manufacturer of mobile home heating devices. Both companies sold to the same industry, mobile home manufacturers, but in different geographic regions. Now, they can each cross-sell into the other company's existing channels.

In both of these instances, developing new customers by relying on the traditional bag of tricks of sales and marketing would have been a far more cumbersome, expensive, and time-consuming undertaking than was the path chosen.

Less Expensive R & D

Research and development can be both expensive and risky. By buying a smaller company that has already succeeded, you can essentially purchase the R&D that they have already done, without uncertainty about cost, development time, odds of success, or quality of the final product.

For example, we were once retained by two companies that produced software that was used to track building maintenance. The software was complex, covering parts inventory, preventative maintenance, employee timekeeping, response times, and a variety of other items. One company had a large customer base, but old, unattractive software. The other company was a startup, with little revenue but great software. The older company wanted to value the money losing smaller company based solely on the development costs they had incurred, but we showed them that it was worth more than the development cost because the R & D was successfully completed and the product had been robustly tested and proven in the real world. The acquirer argued that they could just spend the same amount of money on development and produce a product that was identical. However, they were eventually convinced that there was a significant chance that if they embarked on the development project on their own they might fail, produce a less attractive product, or go significantly over budget. Additionally, completing a development project from the ground up would take a couple of years. They were buying the most successful developer, and eliminating the risk that they would end up resembling some of the less successful players that they were not even considering purchasing.

Economies of Scale

It is a well-accepted business principle that as volume of sales increases, expenses as a percentage of sales decrease. Fixed expenses such as rent, salaries, insurance, etc., don't change with every additional sale the way variable expenses do. Taking advantage of economies of scale is a clear and common reason for one company to acquire or merge with another company. For example, the owner of a small payroll service company reasoned that his company would be most efficient when its volume was near the capacity of its computer system. After all, most costs were pretty much the same whether the company was operating at 20% or 98% of capacity. Furthermore, the company could grow by about 25% without adding any new personnel, and could grow at least another 75% with the addition of only two full time employees. To take advantage of these and other economies of scale, the owner set a growth goal of 100% over one and one-half years. He expected that this ambitious goal would take not only time, but also sales effort, and a good deal of money. The original plan was to add a full time sales person and to use extensive direct mail advertising to area businesses.

Rather than develop new customers through the usual methods, this firm took advantage of an opportunity to essentially buy customers. It did so by purchasing a company with 60 active payroll accounts. Doing so brought the buying company two-thirds of the way to its goal as soon as the deal was closed. What's more, the buyer anticipated reaching break even in one year, a full 33% faster than the 18 months needed by the originally planned method of growth.

It didn't matter to the buyer that the selling firm was barely breaking even. The two firms could merge and take advantage of synergies. The buyer eventually moved the seller's whole operation into his existing facility, thereby saving on rent and related expenses. Clearly, the newly merged firm enjoyed significant economies of scale, which showed up dramatically on the bottom line.

Production Capabilities

Sometimes, a company will buy a business for its productions capabilities. For example, we recently worked with a company that was marketing specialized steel storage containers that were being produced by them in China on a contract basis. We found them a U.S. based company that was manufacturing a similar steel storage device that was being used for a very different purpose. However, the acquiring company saw that the manufacturing capability of the target firm was quite suitable for its manufacturing needs.

Synergistic Products

A company that is successfully marketing a product or service will sometimes buy a company to gain access to a complimentary product that can be sold to its existing customer base. We currently have a client who makes and distributes baked goods to restaurants. He is looking to purchase a company that makes other types of desserts or related items to add to his current baked goods line.

Favorable Lease

Occasionally, a company will have a long-term lease at below market rates. For example, a retailer may have signed a lease in a less than perfect location. However, the area may have changed for the better due to gentrification, changing traffic patterns, or other evolutionary developments. If you can buy a retail business that has a 15-year lease at $9.00 per square foot, while the other stores in the area are paying $17.00 per square foot, you have the makings of a great business advantage. However, you need to be careful to make sure the lease is transferable. Retaining the lease shouldn't be a problem in the case of a stock sale (see Chapter XI), but check with your attorney before getting too far down the road in buying a business for its lease terms.

Trade Name, Trademark, or Brand Name

Several brands that have little to do with product or even with the company that earned their reputation. Yet they still trade largely and successfully on that reputation. For example, the Cuisanart brand has nothing to do with the food processor that made the name what it is or its founder. The brand name was essentially purchased from the founding company many years ago by Conair Corporation, because that company decided (quite rightly) that the brand name has significant value in the marketplace for high-end kitchen products.

Location

Some businesses are more dependent on location than any other variable. A tourist shop, for example, has few repeat or regular customers. However, shops that sell tourist souvenirs near the Empire State Building or the Eiffel Tower can do very well based on the neverending flow of tourists passing their windows. For many, if not most, retail businesses, location is a key ingredient to success.

Of course, if location is your sole criteria, a business acquisition may not be what you need. You may be in the market for a failing business vacating a good location or an empty space, zoned for the purpose for which you intend to use it.

Diversification of Client Base

Diversifying your client base can reduce the risk and increase the value of your business, especially if your company has a high customer concentration. For example, we were approached by a large non-emergency medical transportation company with operations in three states. They had recently withdrawn from a fourth state, when the method that state used to allocate Medicaid transportation changed, making the business far less lucrative for them. Their strategy was to diversify geographically so that no state would account for more than 20% of their operations. Buying an existing business allowed them to begin operations in a new state with a manager (the former owner of the acquisition target) who knew the regulations in that state, and had an existing client base, a physical location, and a set of employees. Setting up from scratch would have cost them more than the acquisition.

Elimination of Competition

A few years ago, the owner of a convenience store asked us to find a buyer for his business. We didn't have to look far. His only nearby competitors bought the business almost immediately. The new owner closed the door on the store he had just bought, and put up a sign referring customers up the block. Within three months the new owner raised his prices by 10%-20%. The price increase stuck because customers could no longer shop the two competitors for the best prices. While this example is a bit extreme, it is not uncommon for a buyer to buy out a competitor merely to create a less competitive marketplace. See Chapter IV for more information on buying a direct competitor.

Planning the Acquisition

As with all business ventures, careful planning is a key to success. A well-executed acquisition typically includes a good business plan. The only problem here is that a full business plan cannot be prepared until an appropriate acquisition target is found. Obviously, the nature and direction of the target company will impact the business plan.

Before getting to the point of a specific target company and a business plan, a few preliminary steps are in order.

The first step is to clearly define exactly what you want the acquisition to accomplish. Typical acquisition goals include:

- Elimination of competition
- Expansion to new markets
  - Geographic

- ☐ New niche(s)
- Economies of scale in operations
- Economies of scale in marketing
- Economies of scale in other areas
- Acquiring employees with needed talents and skills
- Utilization of excess capacities
  - ☐ New products and services to sell to existing distribution channels
  - ☐ New distribution channels to sell your current products and services (and those of the company being acquired)
  - ☐ Diversification and expansion of customer base
- Growth toward implementation of a profitable exit strategy
- Reduced customer concentration
- A public offering
- A sale at higher multiple (as can be expected for a larger company)

It is unlikely that each of your goals is equally important. For this reason, it's good idea to assign a point value to each of the goals and sub-goals. For example, if your primary goals are to increase distribution channels and diversify your customer base, and your geographic preference is New England, you probably wouldn't want to rule out a company in New York State that otherwise fits your criteria.

Writing down your goals will help considerably in sharpening your focus toward your goal. The time it takes to commit your goals to writing will help you resist the common distraction of looking at companies that are attractive, but inappropriate in that they won't help you achieve your acquisition objectives. We have too often seen strategic buyers spend hours, even days, determining that a particular company won't fit their needs, when a good summary of goals could have shortened the time to minutes.

Acquisition Summary

We recommend that you prepare an acquisition summary that will incorporate your acquisition goals. The summary will contain additional information such as:

- Overview of the buying company
- A somewhat detailed description of the type of acquisition sought
- Size requirements (in volume, number of employees, or other quantifiable criteria)
- Preferred timetable for making an acquisition
- Profitability requirements
- Management requirements
- Geographical requirements
- Outline of your plan to finance the acquisition
- Anything that would make a prospective acquisition company unacceptable to you

This summary will be used for at least two purposes. First, it will help you to clarify your own reasons for pursuing an acquisition and the benefits that you need to gain from that acquisition. Organizing your thoughts and committing them to paper is an essential step towards a realistic evaluation of your plans. You may well find that some of your vague ideas and thoughts either coalesce or fall apart when you are called upon to put them into a well-organized written plan. If they coalesce, great—go forward. If they fall apart, you have spent a few hours to save many more hours of time and many dollars of investment capital that may have gone towards a project of dubious value.

Second, the acquisition summary will serve as a clear communication tool to both intermediaries and prospective acquisition targets. Lawyers, accountants, business brokers and other intermediaries may be in a position to help you find a suitable company. However, if you merely tell them verbally what you are looking for, it will have far less impact than a clear and concise written document. Furthermore, a written summary will demonstrate your seriousness in pursuing this objective.

We get calls all the time from people interested in buying companies. On occasion, we get a written summary that clearly spells out what a prospective buyer is looking for. The verbal request is entered into a database with a brief description. However, the written summary is studied carefully and has a much better chance of being acted upon. Rightly or wrongly, we assume that the person (or company) who provided the written request, even if it is only a page or two long, is a far better prospect because of the effort that went into its preparation.

However, some of these written summaries are so *pie in the sky* that we assign them a low priority. Without exaggeration, we occasionally get acquisitions summaries that detail exemplary requirements like the following:

- Minimum 15% annual growth for past 4 years
- Stable record of net profit of at least 20%
- Audited financials
- Priced at no more than 3.25 times EBITDA
- Owner willing to finance 50% of acquisition price

Such a business would indeed be very attractive. It would be so attractive, in fact, that we would be able to get 3 or 4 offers within a week. That's if we didn't buy it ourselves first.

It is important that your acquisition summary be reasonable. A key purpose of the summary is to encourage possible sellers and intermediaries to be interested in you as an acquirer. Sellers tend to be a bit paranoid about *tire kickers* and of buyers wanting to *steal* the business they worked hard to build. One job of intermediaries is to screen out unrealistic buyers. An acquisition summary that demonstrates unrealistic expectations will surely backfire.

In a way, the roles of buyer and seller are reversed when it comes to acquiring a business. In most buy/sell situations, the buyer has lots of choices, so the burden is on the seller to convince that buyer to go with his offer over the others. When buying a computer, a car, or a television, there are a huge variety of good choices. However, the supply of good businesses for sale or even potentially for sale is quite limited. To a degree, the acquirer is in the role of persuading the seller that he (or his company) is the best buyer, the best caretaker and nurturer, for that seller's company.

For this reason, gaining the seller's trust and confidence is important. Your acquisition summary should include information about your own company's background and plans regarding acquisition. The seller wants to know that the company he built will be well taken care of going forward. It is at least equally as important that the seller or intermediary be assured that your company has the financial capability to facilitate an acquisition and bring it to a successful close. While a seller undoubtedly will have signed a non-disclosure agreement before a face-to-face meeting, reiterating your company's commitment to strict adherence of the terms of that agreement will be reassuring to a jittery seller.

We deal extensively with private equity groups (PEGs). These PEGs are in the business of acquiring and growing companies on behalf of investors who have provided them with capital to deploy. The more successful of these professional buyer groups take great care to build a relationship with potential seller based on mutual trust and confidence from the very beginning of discussions. Some PEGs insist on meeting sellers for lunch or dinner for a get-to-know each other session before actually talking about specific business and financial issues. In competitive buying situations, we have seen this relationship building approach pay dividends in that the seller develops a clear preference for one buyer over another, and that buyer has the inside track when proposals are submitted. The reverse is also true: a buyer that fails to develop sellers' trust is taken far less seriously and goes to the bottom of the list of preferred acquirers.

III. Finding Acquisition Targets

Let's oversimplify things a bit and divide all businesses into three groups:

- Group One: Those businesses that are actively for sale.
- Group Two: Those businesses that are not actively for sale but may be open to seriously exploring the possibility of being acquired.
- Group Three: Those businesses that absolutely are not for sale.

In this section we'll first discuss Group One, and then Group Two. Businesses in Group Three may eventually move to Group One or Two.

Businesses Actively for Sale

In most circumstances, someone who wants to sell something will try to get the word out and promote that product or service he wants to sell. In selling one's company, this isn't always the case because putting a business on the market can cause concern among customers and employees. Many business owners want to sell, but are also very concerned about keeping the intent to sell as confidential as is possible. That being the case, finding businesses that are for sale often involves a few steps such as talking to an intermediary, signing a non-disclosure agreement, providing information about yourself or your company, and getting "screened in" by the seller or the seller's representative. Ads and announcements of businesses for sale are often long on generalities, but purposefully lacking in identifying details. The methods below are useful as a first step in finding opportunities, best described as getting leads for possible acquisition targets. Be understanding about the seller's concerns about confidentiality and discretion, and be prepared to jump through a few hoops before receiving the details that you need to decide if you are seriously interested in a particular acquisition opportunity.

Business for Sale Websites

There are several websites that specialize in listing businesses for sale that allow you to search by type, size, geography, and more. Some of the better-known business-for-sale websites include:

www.bizbuysell.com

www.businessmart.com

www.mergernetwork.com

www.bizquest.com

While the chances of finding a company on one of these sites that meet your defined acquisition needs is not that great, these sites, and others like them, are worth a look. In fact, it's worth looking at them once a week or more often because new offerings are added regularly. Some of these sites can save your search and send you an email if and when a match comes up. Some people have developed their own search tools that automatically search these sites as often as a couple times a day in the hope that a company meeting their specific criteria will appear and they'll be able to act on it right away.

These sites tend towards listing very small companies—those with sales of under about $1.5 million—but there are also larger companies listed.

Other Web-Based Searching

Many brokers and intermediaries list the companies they are currently representing for sale in a way that Google or other search engines can find them. Also, some business owners set up their own websites to advertise their company for sale. It is certainly worthwhile to try a few search engine searches in the hope that your ideal acquisition opportunity will turn up.

As part of our business brokerage activities, we have developed proprietary tools that search for businesses for sale, both on the web and in proprietary databases. There may be other business brokers that have developed similar proprietary tools.

Classified Ads in Newspapers

Even with the advent of the web and its arguably superior ability to handle the function of classified advertising, there are still newspapers, and those newspapers still run classified ads. Many papers include a "Businesses for Sale" or "Business Opportunity" section in their classified sections. As with web-based business for sale sites, chances of finding your ideal strategic acquisition candidate are not that great. However, classified sections of local newspapers are worth a look, especially if you are looking for a small company within one or a few local markets.

If you are looking for a larger acquisition candidate(s), your best bet is *The Wall Street Journal*. Its classified section, called "The Mart," includes a subsection called "Businesses for Sale". Thursday has the most extensive business for sale listings. However, even on Thursdays, the Businesses for Sale section of this newspaper has far fewer ads than in years past. Note that for *The Wall Street Journal*, advertisers can limit their ads to various regions of the country, so if you're looking to buy a company in, say, northern California, don't look at a *Wall Street Journal* purchased in Connecticut.

Brokers and other Intermediaries

Very few brokers will aggressively search for a business for sale for a particular seller. The reason is simple. It is generally far more profitable for a broker to try to sell a business than to try to find one that a buyer will buy. To understand why, put yourself in the broker's shoes. Let's assume that both a business owner who wants to sell and one who wants to buy approach a broker and ask for his assistance. First, the broker needs to assess the probability that each will consummate a transaction. There are many more active buyers than sellers at most times, so the odds are higher that a seller will succeed in selling than the buyer will succeed in buying, but for the sake of argument let's assume here that the broker believes that each of the two business owners has a 90% chance of completing a transaction within the next year.

The seller will almost certainly be willing to sign an exclusive deal with the broker, giving the broker a 90% chance of collecting his commission. The buyer, however, will almost certainly want to preserve the right to find a business without the assistance of the broker or with the assistance of another broker. So, while the buyer may have the same odds of closing an acquisition, the broker's odds of collecting a commission might be 20% instead of 90%.

Furthermore, the size of the commission from a seller is fairly predictable, since the broker can value the company before entering into the agreement. However, when working with a buyer the negotiations may be well underway before the broker and the buyer are able to accurately value the acquisition target. It is not unusual to find an acquisition candidate that is willing to talk about selling because they are experiencing financial or other challenges that make the business worth substantially less and have a transaction occur that is well under the anticipated price range.

So, not only does a broker looking on behalf of a seller have a higher chance of collecting a commission than one looking on behalf of a seller, but he is much less likely to have a commission that is substantially lower than anticipated.

Since the incentives to represent a seller are so much higher, intermediaries almost always work for the seller. Therefore, reasonably enough, they sell the companies that they have been hired to represent for sale. If you learn that an intermediary happens to be representing a company that meets your acquisition criteria, by all means check out what that intermediary is offering.

Some buyers contact several intermediaries to apprise them of their acquisition criteria. Other than the time investment, there is certainly no downside in doing this. There is no equivalent to a multiple listing service such as those that exist in the real estate industry, so in most instances, brokers will only know what they and perhaps a few associates have for sale.

Most intermediaries get far more calls from prospective buyers than they do from prospective sellers. Calls from buyers are not always taken all that seriously unless that broker happens to have a listing that matches the buyer's stated criteria.

Evaluating Buyers

Brokers typically have formal and/or informal methods to evaluate and screen prospective buyers to determine which are worthy of taking seriously, and which are unlikely to lead to closing a deal. In general, that criteria is along these lines:

- What is your primary business or your job focus? If you are a private equity group, a representative of a holding company, or a dedicated business development professional at a large company, then you are in the business of buying companies, so you are considered a good candidate for closing a deal.

- If you are the CEO of your business, you have competing priorities. Your existing business's performance needs to take priority over a potential acquisition. Deals sometime fall apart when a person with other, more immediately pressing responsibilities has to slow or suspend the process while they attended to other issues.

- Do you have a history that includes acquisitions? A company that has grown through acquisition in the past is more likely to close a deal than one that has not.

- Do you have funding, a reasonable record of obtaining funding for acquisitions in the past, or at least knowledge of how to obtain funding? During the acquisition process the likelihood that you will complete a deal will repeatedly be evaluated. If you have funding in place, brokers and potential sellers will take you more seriously.

- How professional is your appearance? Do you have a website, business cards, and the other accoutrements of a business? Are they really slick and well-designed, or do they look thrown together? Is your demeanor on the phone and in person polite and professional? These things may be entirely superficial, but there is no question that they will affect how others assess you, and therefore affect your chances of completing an acquisition.

- How well can you articulate what you are searching for? If you can't clearly explain what you are looking for, then you will be taken less seriously and you will waste time performing poorly defined searches and evaluating acquisition candidates that you decide are not a good fit. Hint: never tell a broker "I'm open to any kind of business". If you do, you'll be perceived as a dreamer who hasn't thought this through.

- How easy will it be to find a good acquisition candidate? If you are looking to approach, say, building maintenance services in the Dallas Fort-Worth area, they are relatively easy to identify and evaluating them is fairly straightforward. On the other hand, we recently did a search for a company that was looking for newly developed disposable products used in radiology that could be marketed using a telemarketing strategy. They wanted only products that had a significant demonstrable advantage over market-leading products. Identifying companies with products that fit their description was very difficult.

Acquisition Search Services

Some brokers, ourselves included, will do searches on behalf of buyers on a fee or fee plus small commission upon closing basis.

If you are looking for a very specific kind of business, such as one to synergistically compliment your existing business, a search service is worth considering. While brokers will be more than willing to sell what they have available for sale, they will be far less willing to do a comprehensive search or to contact specific companies in the hope that they can persuade one to sell. Many of the brokers that will search on behalf of buyers are less concerned with producing results for the buyers than they are in using the search as a way to generate new sell side listings. Hence, they will nominally search for an acquisition candidate for you, but in reality cast a wide net, talking to many businesses that fall outside of your target criteria in an attempt to get a foot in the door that they can turn into a lucrative sell-side listing. In the absence of a contract that grants you first refusal, if they do find a sellable company that looks great, they may present it not just to you, but also to a number of their other buy side contacts in the hopes of raising the odds that a deal happens. They may overlook potential targets that produce too small a commission for them but would help achieve your goals. The broker has a financial interest in seeing a large sale completed, not in getting you the best possible deal.

On the other hand, a good search service has processes in place to find companies that meet specified criteria, approach their owners, and bring those owners who have not yet put their company up for sale to the table. Information on our acquisition search service is available on our website strategic-acquisitons.com/buyers-advantage/.

Attorneys, Accountants, and Consultants

Lawyers and accountants, and some consultants by nature of the work they do, have inside knowledge of what is going on with their client's businesses. A lot of business owners consult their lawyer or accountant early on, when they are considering a sale. So, telling your own lawyer and accountant as well as other lawyers and accountants who you may know that you are looking to acquire a business just might lead to learning about a company for sale that meets your criteria.

Trade Publications & Associations

Some sellers will advertise their business for sale in trade and professional publications. In our experience, this avenue tends to be limited to smaller companies, but a quick look is certainly worth the effort. Expect trade publication business for-sale ads to be particularly oblique. Sellers are rightly concerned that their trade publication may well be read by their employees and their competitors.

More than occasionally, trade associations get inquiries from members who are interested in buying or selling their businesses. Some trade associations are very good about assisting with acquisition opportunities. We have been invited many times to give presentations about buying and selling companies at industry conventions because members have asked for information on the subject. Your trade or professional association is worth contacting about your acquisition interest.

Gray Area Sellers

A few businesses are actively on the market and may be found by the methods outlined above. While you might find a few good acquisition candidates in the pool of businesses that are listed for sale, the odds of doing so are not great. What's more, once a desirable business is actively advertised for sale, it will attract several qualified buyers leading to significant competition among the suitors.

There are a lot of business owners that aren't actively looking to sell, but would consider selling under the right circumstances. We call these the gray area sellers. It is among these gray area sellers where we believe the best strategic acquisition opportunities lie.

Finding these gray area sellers is not easy. In chapter VI we will outline the emotional attachment many entrepreneurs have with their business. Selling one's business is an emotionally wrenching undertaking, such that even an owner considering selling will not always readily respond to a query about selling.

Since we specialize in finding these gray area sellers, we have a great deal of experience in finding and arranging the purchase of businesses that aren't officially for sale. Our methods involve the proverbial mix of science and art, so it's difficult to lay out a procedure in a recipe-like format. Having said that, here are some of the methods we have found to be successful over time.

Direct Approach via Traditional Mail

Now that communications methodologies like instant messaging, texting, and Tweeting are commonplace, even email seems almost old-fashioned. Sending a paper letter by first class seems particularly antiquated to some. Nevertheless, this is still one of our main methods of finding leads for gray area sellers.

Yes, we still often use first class letters that are hand-stamped and hand-signed in our initial effort to locate acquisition opportunities for our clients. It's not just that we are old-fashioned. We have tested other methods and varied our approach, but have come back to snail mail as a very effective tool for this type of endeavor.

Our search letters are very pinpointed by industry, size, geography, and more. We use the list services of a few companies that enable a user to do this pinpointing and list-buying online. One source we use is InfoUSA, and another is Hoovers. The former company compiles its lists from Yellow Page listings and the latter uses D&B information (D&B is their parent company). We also use Thomas' Register (ThomasNet.com). ThomasNet is not really designed for this purpose, but in some circumstances it is quite usable for certain very specific industry segments. Links to these websites can be found on our website http://strategic-acquisitions.com.

Our letters are always addressed directly to the owner(s) or CEO, and the envelope is always marked "confidential." We always make clear that we are not fishing for a listing, nor seeking a fee. Our most effective letters explain, in detail, what our buyer is looking for. Business owners are accustomed to getting solicitations with vague promises of generous buyers for their businesses, but the brokers either ask for large upfront fees before those buyers are revealed or just ask for a blanket listing agreement. We need to differentiate our letters from those shady solicitations.

Finally, we always promise discretion and confidentiality, even to the extent that we won't share sensitive information with our client company without their permission. This is a key point: if business owners who are actively selling their companies are concerned about confidentiality (and they are), those who are at the *just might consider it* stage are doubly as concerned about their customers, competitors, and employees learning that a sale is being contemplated.

This direct mail approach is cumbersome and expensive. Not only do the letters have to be printed and folded, signed, stamped, and stuffed in envelopes, but there is also time needed for record-keeping of the responses and follow-up needs, as well as, of course, the time to hold conversations with the potential sellers. In an age of electronic communications, it is comparatively very slow. We do it for one key reason: it gets results. It's not magic; depending on the industry, we often consider a response rate of 2% pretty good, and that's a *willing to talk* response, not necessarily a seller. But in the sensitive area of approaching business owners about an issue as weighty as selling their business, it works as well as or better than any other method we have tried.

Email

As the availability of appropriate emailing lists improve, email becomes a more viable method of finding gray area business sellers. However, the necessity of reaching the owner directly and the need for confidentiality makes email a less-than-ideal search method. Also, the old fashioned first class letter on quality paper seems to have more impact than does an email, no matter how well it's worded. Email is also often ignored by the receiver both because of the amount of spam received every day, and because it is so easy and inexpensive to send. In fact, a significant percentage of your email inquiries may end up filtered out as spam. However, email is quicker and cheaper than a postal mailing. The list-compiling companies mentioned above offer email lists along with their traditional postal list services.

Networking

It couldn't hurt to get the word out that you are looking to buy a particular kind of company. Sales representatives and vendors make it their business to know what's going on with their customers and may hear of possible opportunities. In all likelihood, a lead from a source like a vendor would be just that: a lead. It would be along the lines of "Joe at ABC has been saying he wants to retire soon so he may be interested in talking" or "Bill at XYZ seems to be spending more and more time away from his business and might be open to discussions."

We have even run into situations where a customer provides a referral. For example, a manufacturer of drawer hardware was selling to a furniture store that sold high-end furniture. The furniture store was providing that hardware to a manufacturer that made a custom line of furniture for the store. The store asked the furniture maker to buy the drawer hardware manufacturer.

In another case, we were retained to sell a manufacturer of gas detection devices. The owner had recently died after a long fight with cancer and the company had to be sold quickly so that highly skilled employees did not lose faith in the company and begin to leave for other opportunities. Boeing was a major customer, purchasing sensors that used intellectual property that would take years and millions of dollars to replicate and recertify. Since Boeing was concerned about losing a sole supplier of a critical component, they actually assisted us by supplying a number of companies interested in purchasing our client (though ultimately it was sold to a private equity group).

Why Phone Calls Often Don't Work

We have tried using telephone calls to solicit potential sellers. These seldom succeed unless we have a pre-existing relationship with the seller. Unfortunately, when you call a potential seller, you not only run the risk of interrupting him when he is doing a more pressing task, but you also often trigger an almost reflexive no. After all, he just received a surprise phone call from somebody that he does not know asking him a highly charged question: "Do you want to sell your business?"

Private Equity Groups

Private equity groups (PEGs) are in the business of buying companies, improving them and enhancing their value, and then reselling them or exiting them through a public offering.

If you are looking for a relatively large company to acquire, private equity groups are a source to look to. You are unlikely to find bargains, but you will find sophisticated and rational dealmakers who are more than willing to talk to you.

A good, though expensive, source to search for private equity owned companies by industry and company type is

www.privateequityinfo.com.

Intermediaries

Unlike most intermediaries, we focus on aggressively searching for synergistic acquisitions targets for our clients. We maintain a comprehensive database of inquiries we receive from owners who are considering selling, but haven't pulled the trigger yet. We have also developed some proprietary technology that efficiently searches other intermediary sites, business for sale sites (such as bizbuysell.com), private equity sites, and other sources based on our client's acquisition criteria.

Summary

At any given time, a few businesses are actively on the market. Also at any given time, there are some businesses, those we term *gray area sellers*, that are not actively on the market, but may be open to talking about being acquired in whole or part. A strategic buyer looking for a particular type of acquisition is more likely to find it in the second group. There is no magic method for finding the perfect acquisition. However, the methods described above have proven successful in many cases.

IV. Put Your Competitor Out of Business: Buy Them

Special Considerations When Attempting to Buy Your Competitor

How many times have you wondered how much more profitable your business would be if you could only eliminate one or more of your major competitors? Well, you can do it legally, ethically, and efficiently by buying your competitor.

All of the advantages of a strategic acquisition discussed in Chapter II and throughout this book apply, and then some. In buying a direct competitor, you will gain some of these benefits:

- new customers and a more diversified customer base

- market share

- lower marketing costs

- enhanced pricing power

- economies of scale and elimination of redundancies

- new distribution channels

- new production capabilities

- synergistic products

- a new trademark(s), trade name(s), and/or brand name(s)

- favorable location(s)

- new skilled employees

- new products or product lines

- new design and development capabilities

Most importantly, you can gain very real additional advantages if your major competitor is suddenly no longer a competitor, but instead a new division of your company!

You can make 2 + 2 = 5

Buying a competitor can be quite a business coup. While there are special advantages in buying a direct competitor, there are special difficulties as well. It is not easy to approach a competitor, even a friendly competitor, with a proposal so bold as a buyout. If you were to directly approach your competitor with such a proposal, the likely knee-jerk answer would be "NO." Even if the answer was more along the "I'll think about it" lines, once that competitor thought about how he'd have to share intimate financial and other details about his business with a competitor in the course of trying to complete a deal, the answer would still likely be a no.

You can't blame your competitor for being especially sensitive, even to the point of suspicious, to an inquiry from a direct competitor. If the situation were to be reversed, if your competitor were to ask you about selling your business to him, you would be very apprehensive as well.

So how do you get a buyout conversation going with your competitor? The initial approach, always important when persuading a business owner to consider a sale, is doubly important when it comes to approaching a competitor. In this chapter, we'll explain our method for doing this on behalf of clients, and explain a few mistakes to avoid.

We'll also talk about other strategic acquisition issues that pertain specifically to buying one's competitor, including valuing a competitor's business, obtaining financing, and what to do if your get a "No."

One word of caution: There are strict federal anti-trust and restraint of trade laws designed to prevent reduction of competition that can be construed as harmful to consumers. As a practical matter, it is highly unlikely that these laws would come into play for small to mid-size businesses. These are typically at issue in the case of very large companies. However, if acquiring a competitor might result in significantly limiting competition in a particular marketplace, run it by your attorney before getting too far down the road toward that acquisition.

Approaching Your Competitor about Acquisition Talks

Before even making the approach, we recommend a Pre-approach:

First Do Your Homework.

At the outset, gather information about your competitor. Even if you don't close a deal, it's always good to have solid information about your competition. You can get a wealth of information from some of these sources:

- Vendors and Suppliers: Vendors tend to know a good deal

about their customers, and are often willing to share what they know. A simple question or two like "Hey, how's Bob Smith doing? I haven't spoken to him for a while" may result in useful new information.

- Database Information: A lot of third party information is available via the Internet, though not necessarily for free. The information available varies but typically includes information regarding:

  o Estimated credit worthiness

  o Number of employees

  o Sales volume

  o Owner and/or CEO's name

  o Public filings

  o Legal issues

  o Liens and, to a degree, creditors and other information on loans

  o Other things that you probably already know like the company's address, website, phone number, etc.

Here are some of the sources we use to gather information about a particular company:

- Dunn & Bradstreet (D&B, dandb.com): D&B is by far the most venerable and arguably the best source of information about pretty much any US based company. However, unless you subscribe to D&B, their reports are quite expensive. As of this writing, a standard business report from D&B for a single business is priced at $122.00.

- Credit.net: This database offers pretty good information on individual companies, though not as complete (and probably not as accurate) as D&B. It's offered on a subscription basis. However, you can sign up for a free seven-day trial, more than enough time to get the file on a competitor or two.

- Experian (http://sbcr.experian.com/): Experian is another credit bureau that offers information files on many US businesses. While their reports may not be as complete and up to date as D&B, they are pretty good, and a single report (called a "Profile Plus Report") is priced at about $50 as of this writing.

- A to Z (atozdatabases.com): This service provides basic information about many businesses. It's marketed primarily to libraries that turn around and offer it free to their patrons. If you have access to a library that subscribes to A to Z, it's well worth taking a look at your competitor's file, though it won't be as extensive as the paid services.

- Secretary of State (where business is located): Many states now put their database of corporations and LLCs online, generally for free. You can look up your competitor's state filings. However, you won't get a whole lot of information other than officers' names, whether the company is owned by another company, and whether its state filings are current.

Broaching the Subject of Buying Your Competitor

The initial approach to your competitor about buying his or her business is as tricky as it is critical. For many business sellers, the sale of the business he or she built is as much an emotional decision as it is a financial one. The idea of selling to a direct competitor is even more emotionally wrenching. The wrong approach can poison the atmosphere for good.

Be Sensitive

In broaching the subject, be sensitive to the emotions as well as the genuine risk your competitor faces in disclosing proprietary information to you. Understand that while your intentions may be honorable and you believe your proposal is in your competitor's best interest, he or she will be suspicious and guarded.

Chapter VII of this book talks about seller psychology. Reread it before making your approach, and understand that competitors are even more sensitive and suspicious than business owners in general.

Once you've reread Chapter VI, start with a carefully worded and polite letter or email. If you have a personal relationship with your competitor, start with a phone call if you feel it's appropriate. I generally frown on starting with a phone call unless you know your competitor well, because too often, it results in a knee-jerk "no." A letter or email though gives him or her the opportunity to think about the proposal a bit without committing to a "no," and then feeling he has to keep to what he said in the first place. People accustomed to making decisions, such as business owners, hate to go back on the decision they initially made. In a week or so following the initial contact, follow-up with a phone call, and be as polite as possible.

Mitigate as much risk and resistance as possible right from the start. It may be best to propose a lunch meeting or a drink to discuss "a possible business opportunity for both of us." When you do start talking business, consider using the term merger rather than acquisition or buyout. Don't ask for sensitive financial or other proprietary information right away. In fact, before you do ask for this type of information, offer a written non-disclosure agreement. If you encounter resistance, allow your competitor to anonymize data by calling customers "Customer A," "Customer B," etc. Employee data can also be anonymized. After consulting with an attorney you may be able to offer to sign a no cross-hire agreement, which protects you too. Above all, show respect for your competitor; doing otherwise can easily kill any chance of a deal.

Try to create an atmosphere of "we are working together here". Bring up the possibility of your competitor working with you (for you) as part of the deal. You will probably need him to make for a smooth transition, to retain customers, and to calm the fears of nervous employees. Even if you are a far better manager and run a more successful company than he does, you still will likely learn a few things from him about the business you're buying and the marketplace it serves. Beyond the practical transition and operational benefits, recognizing his value shows the kind of respect that may alleviate his resistance to discussing the possibilities.

A Little Gentle Pressure

Be polite and put your competitor at ease, but tactfully sprinkling in some discussion about the downside of not selling may help if the prospective seller is a fence-sitter.

Your Plans to Grow

You don't want to make a threat like "Well, if you don't sell, I'm going to double my marketing and take away half of your customers." Yes, we've heard buyers say things like that. However, you may talk about your intent to grow your company, preferably by acquisition, but by other means if a mutually beneficial acquisition can't be worked out.

Mutual Enemies Make Mutual Friends

My father owned an independent drug store. He competed with three or four other independent drug stores in the area. While they were competitors, they bonded over a bigger threat than one another: the big chain pharmacies like CVS and Walgreens.

If your target competitor and you share a common threat, feel free to talk about that. It doesn't have to be a scarier competitor. It can be technological advances that are radically changing your industry, or possible new government regulations, or changes such as a major regional employer shutting down that may affect the entire community. If there are potential threats, gently exploit them to inject some doubt into your competitor's mind about remaining in business. Again, if he is a fence-sitter, your job is to make him understand the tough road he faces if he continues running his business instead of selling to you.

If You Get a 'No'

Despite your best efforts, you may well end up with a "no." Selling one's business is a difficult and emotional undertaking for any owner, especially when the potential buyer is a competitor.

If you do get a "no," try to keep the door open. Whatever you do, don't alienate your potential seller with a statement like "Well, I'll put you out of business anyway," or "You're making a big mistake." You see, it may not be a hard "no." Your approach may have jogged his or her thinking about selling, and in a few weeks or months, that "no" may change to a "maybe" or even a "yes." You want to be able to come back later and try again, so don't spoil your chances of making a deal in the future by making statements that show anything other than a desire to work together and continuing to be cordial.

Try something non-threatening like, "I understand. I wish you the best of luck. Let's keep in touch." I would advise a call every few months for as long as you're interested in the possibility of acquisition. In many, if not most instances, the decision to sell is made after a period of time and some reflection. Business owners, especially as they approach retirement age, mull the possibility of selling with their willingness to sell going back and forth between yes and no over a period of months or years. You want to be there when his thinking has evolved to the point that he is ready to consider selling, and before he actually puts the company on the market.

Approach a Different Competitor?

Once you have some experience with approaching competitors, perhaps there is another one to approach about a buyout. Sure, you may have had your heart set on Competitor A, and though he said no, you are taking our advice and planning to call him again in a couple months. In the meantime, it might be worth considering Competitor B or Competitor C.

There may even be competitors, albeit it less direct ones, that you are less familiar with because they are in a different geographic region or use different sales and distribution channels. Take a look at Chapter III on finding businesses for sale. See if any of the methods detailed there might be worth your consideration.

What's a Merger?

Buyers often refer to acquisitions as mergers for a number of reasons. These include the fact that many business owners dislike the idea of being acquired, since it conjures images of loss of control, loss of employment, and even of failure. Using the softer term, merger, when referring to a transaction may also allay some concerns among customers and employees.

Any transaction in which owners of both entities end up with equity can be referred to as a merger. However, real mergers are rare and mergers of equals are even rarer. In fact it is widely believed that the largest "merger of equals" of all times was really nothing of the sort, and that portraying it as such contributed to its failure to thrive. Here's the way that ABC News explained it:

It was supposed to be a perfect union of carmakers.

When the two companies merged in 1998, Daimler Chairman Juergen Schrempp promised a "merger of equals." But it wasn't long before Chrysler executives complained the bullheaded Germans wouldn't listen to the Americans.

A link to the complete article can be found on our website: http://strategic-acquisitions.com.

In fact, unless both owners end up with 50% of the equity, which is rare, there are no mergers of equals. Few sophisticated buyers will purchase less than 51% of a company, and few sellers are willing to retain a substantial amount of equity unless they can maintain majority ownership. The sad reality is that there are few protections for minority shareholders in closely-held companies. The majority shareholder can hire himself and his family members with generous compensation, he can engage in transactions with other entities that he controls, and so on in order to redirect profits to himself.

The exception to this rule is for venture capital firms and private equity groups. They are sometimes willing to buy less than 50%, and management is often willing to retain less than 50% equity in transactions with these kinds of companies. The reason is that PEGs and VCs buy with the intention of growing the company and exiting the business in three to five years.

A PEG or VC has a big incentive not to play games and reduce apparent profits—they want to maximize the price that they receive for the company when they flip it. PEGS and VCs are also in the business of buying other companies and have a reputation to uphold. If a PEG buys a majority share in a company and treats the sellers, who retain a minority interest, badly, then they will find it harder to convince other sellers to retain an interest, since sellers often talk to the management of companies already in the portfolio of a PEG to which they are considering selling. Management in a company that has a PEG or VC as an investor has the same incentive. Nevertheless, when we've seen offers from PEGs that are willing to purchase a minority interest in a closely held company, they often contain strong protections for the minority shareholder, including the right to force the sale of the entire company to a third party.

That is not to say that a transaction cannot contain an equity component for the seller. A seller may be willing to retain a small equity position (perhaps 5%). This small share of equity can be used as a way to bridge a gap between the seller and the buyer. It may be attractive from a buyer's perspective too, since it is essentially owner financing the cost of which is directly related to the success of the business.   Having the owner retain equity can also be a strong motivator if the owner will be joining the management team of the acquirer.

One structure in which the seller retains equity is the leveraged recapitalization. In a leveraged recapitalization, the company being sold takes a loan for the majority of the purchase price, the new owners put in some equity capital, and the existing owners retain an equity stake. For example, a company valued at $10,000,000 might be recapitalized as follows:

Existing owner's equity capital:	1,000,000
New owners' equity capital:	1,500,000
Bank Loan:	7,500,000
Total Capital:	10,000,000

The existing owners retain 40% of the equity in the company, but pocket 9,000,000 in cash (less transaction costs and taxes, of course). The owners then grow the business and exit by selling (usually in 3 to 5 years).

There are, of course, issues with this deal structure, such as the ability of the business to repay the loan from cash flow, maintaining adequate capital to grow the business, how well existing owners and new owners can work together, the skills that each party brings to the table, and how major decisions are made. An owner who wants to take money off the table, however, can take a lot of money out of the business while maintaining significant upside potential and gaining a new partner that brings skill and capital to the table.

Using An Intermediary

Approaching a direct competitor is often best done through an intermediary. An intermediary versed in strategic acquisition can add a level of protection by promising discretion and by assuring all non-disclosure agreements and procedures are followed. The fact that an intermediary has been retained will indicate to your target competitor that the inquiry is a serious one, not a fishing expedition or an attempt to gain information through subterfuge. Sometimes a competitor may be willing to answer a few questions from an intermediary in order to satisfy their curiosity about who is looking for acquisitions, and once the conversation is started, it is easier to maintain momentum.

An intermediary can be particularly helpful in convincing a competitor of the advantages to him of taking the inquiry seriously, the main one being that his business may well have more value to a competitor than to any outside buyer.

Finally, a good intermediary will have a big *bag of tricks* for putting a deal together. Business buy-sell is a relatively complex endeavor. An intermediary will be able to recommend strategies for bridging gaps, and overcoming a myriad of obstacles that can and will come up that otherwise could kill a deal.

Valuation: Special Considerations When Buying a Competitor

Business valuation is about predicting future performance of a business, and deriving a value that produces an appropriate return on the buyer's investment once it takes into account the measure of risk associated with the business. Most methods of valuation for privately held companies rely on past financial performance as the key predictor of future performance. In most cases, the principle of basing a valuation on past earnings, with certain other factors, makes perfect sense. Chapter VII of this book discusses valuation in detail including the *Excess Earnings* Method, which we generally favor in performing business valuations.

As good as the excess earnings method and the other methods that rely on past earnings may be, they often don't tell the whole story when it comes to buying out a competitor. The overall benefits of buying a competitor are based at least partially on synergies. Yes, the buyer will pick up much of the customer base and cash flow from the company being acquired, but he or she will likely also pick up other benefits that result in more income and lower expenses, including:

- pricing power

- economies of scale

- elimination of redundancies

- market share

- new distribution channel

- production capabilities

For example, suppose you own an IT company. You are renting an office for $1,200 per month. You buy a competing IT company also paying $1,200 per month for office space. You move the acquired company's two employees into your existing office space. As soon as the lease on the acquired company's office is up, you save $1,200 each month; over $14,000 per year falls to your bottom line. Valuation methods that rely principally on past earnings would not account for this kind of savings.

Another example: Let's assume again that you own a small IT company that acquired a competitor that had two employees, bringing your total payroll to five. You've been using an outside payroll service that charges a fixed monthly fee plus a small increment for each employee. The increment goes up for each of the two new employees, but the monthly fixed fee stays the same. In and of itself, this is a very small savings, but similar savings apply to other services you are using that don't need to be duplicated.

One final example: Let's say your software company and your former competitor were both serving the same market: local accounting firms. Though there are other software companies in your community, your competitor and you were the only companies specializing in servicing accounting firms, and the quality of both company's services was perceived to be equal. To be competitive, you had to keep your prices at the same level as your competitor. Now you can raise your prices, as you don't have to worry about losing business to your rival. Again, valuation methods that rely on past earnings don't account for synergies like increased pricing or purchasing power.

Enter: The Discounted Cash Flow Method of Valuation

When valuing a company for an arm's length transaction, almost all sophisticated buyers use past performance as the baseline for future expectations, except in extraordinary circumstances. When valuing a small to midsize business in an arm's length transaction, we generally use the Excess Earnings Method. Valuation in arm's length transactions is covered in detail in Chapter VII. By doing an excess earnings valuation, you get an idea of what the business might sell for if it were being sold to a financial buyer.

However, purchasing a competitor is, in our opinion, the kind of extraordinary circumstance that often merits a different valuation method. We believe that it makes sense to also evaluate the value of the company based on forecasting its future cash flows. Once you forecast the future cash flows, you'll need to discount those cash flows back to their present value, using the Discounted Cash Flow (DCF) method.

The DCF method of valuation considers the value of a projected stream of income adjusted (discounted) for a) the present value of future income, taking the time value of money into account, and b) the estimated risk that the stream of income will materialize as projected.

For example, suppose an investor were offered a payment of $10,000 per year for 10 years. Yes, it adds to $100,000, but no investor would pay $100,000 for that stream of income. An investor would want to consider:

- How much risk is there that he or she won't get all payments in full and on time?

- What is the *opportunity cost* of investing $100,000 today in alternative investments of equivalent risk?

- What are the chances that money will be tied up when it is wanted for something else? How long will it take to free the money up? (liquidity risk)

DCF methodology is explained in detail, in Chapter VII.

DCF vs. Excess Earnings Method of Valuation

The DCF valuation establishes what the maximum value of the business is to you. Your goal is to buy the company as cheaply as possible, but most strategic buyers end up paying a small premium (10-15%) over the price that a financial buyer might pay.

As an example, let's say that the company you want to acquire has a value of $1,500,000 based on an excess earnings calculation and a value of $2,250,000 based on discounted cash flow. A final sale price of $1,650,000 would represent a premium of 10% to the seller, but still be $600,000 less than the company's anticipated value to you. The DCF valuation establishes an absolute cap on what you should pay for the acquisition.

Create Detailed Projections to Use DCF

Bear with us, this get a bit technical.

Two Sets of Projections

You will need to create two sets of projections to do this analysis correctly. The first projection is for your company alone (assuming that no acquisition is made) over the next few years. First you need to decide how far into the future you can accurately project income and expenses. It is possible that you already have a budget or other projection for part or all of the period in question. Some companies don't have an internal budgeting/forecasting process in place. If you don't have a forecasting process, start with your latest income statement.

First: Forecast Income

Begin by forecasting income (sales). You can look at historic sales growth rates, contracts in place (where applicable), and sales in the pipeline. For retail establishments it is important to consider lease expiration and seasonality. Make sure to take into account the possibility that expiring contracts will not be renewed or will be reduced. Remember that not all sales in the pipeline will be realized, and that the percentage of sales that close may be lower (or higher) than the historic rate.

If you cannot create a detailed forecast for the entire period of time that integrating the new acquisition will take, you can use historic company or industry growth rates.

Consider the Effect of Capital Purchases

Any planned capital expenditures should be noted and their effects on sales estimated. Remember that for discounted cash flows we are forecasting based on actual cash flows, not based on accrual accounting. Hence, equipment and other assets are not capitalized, and we disregard depreciation and amortization.

Forecast Expenses

Next, forecast expenses. You need to look at contracts that may have price changes built in (such as leases) and estimate new pricing on contracts that will be renewed or replaced in the time period under consideration. Look at expenses as either fixed, semi-fixed, or variable, and adjust the semi-fixed and variable costs based on projected sales volumes. As discussed above planned capital expenditures are important because they affect cash flows and sales, but they also can affect expenses. Cost of Goods Sold may be reduced by capital expenditures that increase labor productivity or reduce energy use and/or material waste.

Create Projections for the Combined Company

Next, you need to create another set of projections for the combined companies. Start with the latest income statements from both entities. Project sales for both companies. You need to combine forecast sales for the combined company. You may then be able to add to the combined sales figure for several reasons. First, it is possible that you will be able to reduce the overlap in sales efforts, allowing your sales force to reach more customers. Of course, realigning sales territories is not easy and takes time.

You may also be able to sell products that you offer and the acquisition target does not offer to the target's current customer base and products that the acquisition target offers which you do not to your current customer base. However, be careful not to overestimate the ability to cross-sell We have seen buyers that were over-optimistic about the ability to cross-sell and consequently overpaid for an acquisition. For example, in one acquisition a maker of pre-printed forms bought a software company, assuming that if the software came out of the box preconfigured to align with all of the pre-printed forms they would be able to sell forms to the software company's clients. Unfortunately, the customers already had relationships with printers and were, for the most part, unwilling to switch vendors.

An acquisition may also allow you to compete for larger or more complex projects if prior to an acquisition, you did not have all of the technical expertise or manpower necessary for some projects. An acquisition can broaden the range of engineering talent, testing equipment, construction equipment, etc. that allows you to bid on projects that previously would have been out of reach.

Consider Synergies

You also need to examine the expenses after closing. Start with the income statements for both entities and then adjust for items that will change when the two entities are combined such as:

Labor costs

Post-closing there may be opportunities to reduce labor costs. For example, you may have two CFO's post-closing but need only one. The owner of the selling entity may be retiring. You need to approach this adjustment carefully. Laying off employees risks losing institutional knowledge, customer goodwill, and employee morale. You may want to budget for a period of overlap and severance packages.

Economies of Scale

Combining operations may allow you to buy materials in greater volume at a lower unit cost. It may also allow you to reduce the cost of professional services such as accounting, payroll, legal, marketing and advertising, and information technology costs. Carefully examine the income statement and see where expenses may be reduced. One very common synergy is the ability to combine operations and reduce the real estate required to run the business. Another synergy involves an increase in the utilization rate of machinery and equipment.

Consider Integration Costs

When you acquire another company in addition to savings, there are inevitably costs to integrate the two companies. These include items such as labor costs for the time used to decide which business methods to use (where business methods differ) and to train personnel about new methods and new products and services, conversion of data to consolidate computer systems, customer communication (especially regarding changes to the company name or in which personnel are servicing their account), legal fees for items such as lease assignment, and so forth. Of course, the legal costs related to the acquisition are also a negative cash flow and should be factored into your calculation.

Consider Capital Investments

If you are projecting increased sales from cross selling, opening new markets, or from reducing overlapping sales efforts you need to forecast when you will need to invest in production facilities and equipment to meet the increased demand. This additional investment is a negative cash flow.

Caution: Be Realistic

Be careful when you do your projections. It is easy to paint an overly optimistic picture of the post-closing performance. You may lose business if customers are uncertain, especially if there are personnel changes. Competitors may specifically target your customers. As discussed previously, cross selling can be less effective than you expect. We would advise going over your projections with a consultant who will be less emotionally invested in the acquisition than you are. One possible way to insulate yourself from over optimism is to structure part of the payment for the business based on customer retention or based on an earn out.

Calculate Present Value of Income Stream

Once you have projections of cash flows, you need to calculate the present value of those cash flows. You will do the calculation twice and get two different values, the present value of your business without the acquisition and the value of the combined businesses. You then subtract the present value of your business from the present value of the combined businesses to arrive at the maximum value of the acquisition to you.

Negotiations

Chapter IX covers the process of negotiating the acquisition of a business. There are really only two things to add to that chapter when negotiating with a competitor:

Be Especially Sensitive

As we said (and repeated) in the section of this chapter on approaching your competitor, you need to be particularly sensitive to the prospective seller's point of view and concerns. Be careful: an intended slight or insult can derail negotiations, especially when those negotiations are with an already reluctant and skeptical competitor.

Less Bluster

In a lot of business acquisition negotiations, sellers know little about the buyer, and buyer knows little about the seller. Typically, both sides have a great deal of information that the other side does not have. Seller doesn't know what other acquisition options buyer has, nor what kind of resources they can bring to bear on the sale, nor even what buyer's real intentions are. Buyer may (or may not) know about the industry of the seller's company. But buyer knows little about the seller's business, other than what is presented to them. The buyer is often justifiably concerned that the seller is withholding information.

Now, in the case of one competitor buying another, the information asymmetry is less of a concern. Both sides know the industry, know one another's business, and may know each other personally. It is much harder to pull the wool over the other side's eyes with bluster, threats of other deals in the works, other pending offers, or good or bad changes coming to the industry. So, once you get to the negotiating stage, discussions tend to be cleaner; more business-like, and less theatrical.

Chapter Conclusion

While it may be particularly uncomfortable for two competitors to discuss one buying out the other, it may be well worth the effort. Both parties would share the advantage that the sales process would likely be relatively smooth, and the deal would very likely end in a successful close. After all, buyer and seller may well know one another. Even if that isn't the case, they surely know a lot about one another's business, as they have been directly competing for quite a while. Due diligence would probably be relatively easy given buyer's knowledge, not only of the industry, but of the target company and certainly the marketplace where buyer and seller compete.

So, if there is a chance that a direct competitor of yours may be open to acquisition discussions, it is certainly worth an inquiry. Be understanding of your competitor's apprehensions, but do explain the benefits that would accrue to him.

Finally, given the sensitive nature of approaching a competitor, and the complexity of business valuations and acquisition in general, it may be best to use a third party intermediary versed in this type of deal making.

V. Why Sellers Sell

"Why is the owner selling?" This is often the first question potential buyers will ask. While we don't discount the need to ask this question, we do feel it is given too much importance in the minds of prospective buyers. It is not unusual, nor is it unadvisable, to enter a potential buy/sell situation with a bit of healthy suspicion. More often than not, that suspicion seems to be, "Why does this owner want to sell? Is there a problem with this business that I don't know about? If not, why would he want to sell it?"

The fact is there are myriad reasons why a seller might want to sell. We won't deny for a second that one of those reasons can be that the owner foresees his business is heading for trouble. Probably, the most trusted reason for selling, from a buyer's perspective, is retirement. If a seller says that he is selling because he wants to retire, providing that he is of retirement age, most buyers' suspicions are alleviated. Shrewd sellers, of course, know this, so if they are in their late fifties or older, they may indicate that this is one of the reasons for selling whether or not it is true. Divorce settlements and health problems closely follow retirement as acceptable reasons for selling one's company.

But there are other completely legitimate reasons for selling one's business. Later, we'll present a number of techniques to help you assess the future of a business, regardless of the owner's motivation for selling.

Before getting into reasons for selling, we think it's appropriate to discuss some common misunderstandings about small businesses, and especially about the people who own them. It is these misunderstandings that lead prospective buyers to the erroneous assumption that owners don't sell decent businesses unless they are retiring.

The Glorified Entrepreneur

In recent years the image of the entrepreneur has risen from that of an unscrupulous opportunist to nearly that of a folk hero. No longer are entrepreneurs perceived as con artists who will do just about anything to make a buck. Now they are perceived as innovators, builders, and doers who can overcome all obstacles to attain their company's goals. The companies they start, by popular image, are not sweatshops or amoral entities that exist only to make a profit for their owners. They are instead entities that will help us all transcend the problems of the past and proceed boldly and confidently into the future.

The popular image of today's entrepreneur is that of a well-educated young person tossing aside a hundred career options to pursue a new venture—a new vision. He is tireless, arriving at the office by 6 am and returning home late at night, if at all. During that time this mythical entrepreneur maintains a high level of energy as he wows bankers, investors, and customers, and of course, motivates employees to peak performance. This storybook entrepreneur is fearless in his pursuit of success and will overcome whatever obstacle may be in his path.

In reality, few entrepreneurs fit this romanticized profile. What's more, almost every field has its overachievers. While some entrepreneurs may approach the mythical profile, we're not convinced that small business has any more of a claim to superstars than do law, medicine, sports, or engineering. The vast majority of small business owners are normal people that face the same sets of needs, problems, and life changes as do the rest of us.

Reasons for Selling a Company

The owners of some very well run and profitable companies may, under the right set of circumstances, be willing to sell. Among other things, it depends on their needs and life situations at the time, the offer itself, and the options that the seller perceives for himself. An entrepreneur may consider leaving a good business for the same kinds of reasons that an employee may consider leaving a good job.

Some of the legitimate reasons why sellers sell include:

Retirement

As stated above, retirement is the most acceptable reason for selling a business, in the view of many buyers. While this is a fine reason for selling, don't make the mistake of completely believing a seller who claims retirement plans. Retirement can very easily be the stated reason without being the actual reason.

Often, a retiring owner typically feels little pressure to come to a buy/sell deal. An owner who is looking toward retirement generally does not feel pressure to act quickly. He can decide, "When I'm about 60, I'll start looking at the idea of selling. If it takes three months to find a buyer at my price, that's fine. If it takes three years, that's fine too." A seller in this situation would not be a likely candidate for selling at a bargain price, whereas an owner who is anxious to make a deal quickly might well be willing to listen to a less generous offer.

Take Some Money *Off the Table*

Business involves risk, and small business is particularly risky. While younger entrepreneurs tend to welcome risk, as the years go on, many business owners start thinking more and more about balancing risk with security. A very common reason for wanting to sell at least part of one's business is the need to diversify. Many business owners have most of their net worth tied up in their business. As life circumstances change and time goes on, the desire to lessen risk in favor of security becomes more and more pressing.

For the majority of our deals, this desire to take some money off the table is one of the most important reasons, if not the primary reason, that a seller is considering selling. Deals in which this is one of the key reasons tend to be partial buyouts where the seller may sell 50% to 75% of his company. In some instances, the seller is happy to take some of his payment in the form of shares in the purchasing company.

Owner is Bored or Fed up with the Business

Despite the entrepreneurial myths, many small business owners simply get bored with their businesses. Buyers tend to be especially suspicious of this as a reason for selling. After all, small business is played up to be the greatest most exciting pursuit there can ever be. How is it possible for an owner of a successful business to get bored and give it up? The fact is, it happens. Some people get more of a thrill from starting a business than from running it after the startup phase. Others go into it with misconceptions about what small business ownership entails on a day-to-day basis. The bottom line is that boredom and frustration can occur in small business ownership just as it can in any other career.

A seller recently told us, "I want to sell my company because I've been at it for eight years, and I'm just bored with it. I'm no longer devoting the energy to it that I should be. If my business were failing, I'd have no choice but to get out. Someone can come in here with the energy and enthusiasm that I had when I started the company and grow this business quickly. But I've had it, and I want out." This is not an uncommon sentiment among small business owners despite the lore of the entrepreneur. There are businesses out there with burnt-out owners who don't have the drive or the energy to exploit their company's potential. This kind of company can be a great opportunity for a buyer with the energy and drive to make it happen.

A Good Offer Comes up

Those of us who make part of our living buying and selling businesses sometimes bluntly ask business owners the unsolicited question, "Do you want to sell your company?" A typical response is a long pause followed by a statement of, "Yeah, if the price is right." Small business ownership represents a lot of different things to different people. One thing it represents in nearly all cases is an investment. Many owners reason that if they can earn a good profit by selling that investment, they'll sell it. Clearly, this can be a win-win situation. It is well within the realm of reason to expect that you can get a good deal from a prospective seller, while a seller can earn a profit from the transaction. If this were not the case, our free market system couldn't operate because goods and services couldn't change hands to the mutual advantage of buyers and sellers.

Family Life Changes

Any number of family changes can lead to a decision to sell a company. The birth of a child, an older child going off to college, a divorce, or a death can all lead to a business for sale. While it is not unwise to be suspicious of family changes as reasons for sale, if those changes are believable, they may well be legitimate. Sometimes family changes can put pressure on a seller to sell quickly, which can mean a better negotiating position for you.

Spouse Job Change

It is not uncommon for one spouse to get an out-of-town job offer and for the other to sell his or her business as a result. This situation may mean the seller will be in a hurry to sell and may be willing to consider a lower price. In some unusual cases, part of the job offer may include a stipulation that the employer may compensate the employee (and spouse) for financial loss if the business has to be sold for a lower price than it is worth. In this case, the seller may be even more willing to listen to your low offer, resulting in a bargain opportunity for you. Again, guaranteeing the price of a business by an employer is rare, but not unheard of.

One of the authors sold his business after his wife, a neurology professor, moved from the University of Michigan to Michigan State University. The move meant a 75-mile commute, a situation that became untenable with three young children and with both parents working 60-hour weeks.

Business Owner Gets Job Offer

Conventional wisdom says that no self-respecting entrepreneur would consider working for someone else except under the most dire circumstances. In reality, some entrepreneurs are fence sitters and could be happy either in their own businesses or working for someone else. Entrepreneurs do sometimes get job offers that they consider too good to pass up.

Future Growth Limited by Management Abilities

Recently, we arranged the acquisition of a very successful import company. The selling company was founded by a guy we'll call Frank. Despite the fact that Frank told us himself that he barely made it through high school and had no formal education beyond that, he was one of the smartest business people we've ever met.

A private equity buyer called us with an interest in buying this $12M company. He asked if he could send in a consultant from one of the top consulting firms to evaluate the company on his behalf, as he would be out of the country for several weeks. Of course we agreed.

So, the consultant came down and we gave him the usual tour of the facility. We then retreated to the seller's office to discuss the possibilities. After some initial questions, the conversation went like this:

Consultant: So, tell me Frank, who does your accounting?

Frank: I do. The reason I want to sell this business is that I pretty much do everything myself around here.

Consultant: Uh huh. And you have 30 or so employees. Who is in charge of your HR?

Frank: (looking at him with mild frustration) My what?

Consultant: You know your employees, personnel issues.

Frank: Oh. Like I told you, I do. I handle everything around here. I'm tired of it, and that's why I want to sell.

Consultant: (a few minutes later) Well Frank, you have a very old building here with over 100,000 square feet of space. Tell me, who does your facilities management?

Frank: (At this point he had enough) Look! If the roof is leaking, they call me. If the lights are flickering, they call me. If the toilet is plugged up, they call me. The plunger's right behind your freakin' chair!

At that point the consultant finally got it. Frank's business had no management infrastructure. Frank was stretched too thin. To grow beyond where it was, this company needed a system of management that had better procedures in place and that delegated responsibilities.

For many years, one of our niches has been arranging acquisition deals of successful companies that need to develop a management infrastructure to grow to the next level. A typical situation for us is a company with sales in the $5M to $25M range that is still run by the founding entrepreneur or by the next generation of the founders. Such companies tend to hit a sort of ceiling they can't break through without a systematic management infrastructure that relieves the owner of running every aspect of the company. An owner manager who, as in the example above, is dealing with everything from payroll to personnel issues, and from leaky roofs to plugged-up toilets, has precious little time left to deal with long term or strategic planning.

Companies that fit this profile can be great growth-by-acquisition opportunities, especially if the purchasing company can take over some of the mundane functions that are problematic for the selling company. When, for example, personnel issues can be integrated into a functioning HR Department, and payables and receivable can be integrated into an accounting department, etc., we have the making of a $2 + 2 = 5$ acquisition.

Chapter Summary

Surely there are small business owners who try to unload problematic businesses onto unsuspecting buyers. Buyers are understandably and appropriately suspicious of the reasons that a seller is selling. Buyers are usually most comfortable when the stated reason for selling is that the owner is retiring. The fact is that there are a host of legitimate reasons for a business owner to want to sell; retirement is only one of them. In fact, since shrewd sellers know that buyers like to hear that retirement is the reason for selling, this is sometimes the stated reason even when it is not the actual reason.

If you plan to buy a company, a certain amount of suspicion is well warranted. However, you should spend less effort on deciphering the reason for selling and more on verifying and researching the business—its past and current performance, its prospects, and the seller's claims.

VI. Seller Psychology

Buying a business is an investment. As with any other investment, you need to analytically evaluate an acquisition opportunity in terms of its likely risks and benefits to your company, and determine if it is the most efficient use of available resources to move you toward your stated goals. Unlike with most other business investments, though, you may well have to deal with a seller's emotional issues and vagaries. Many deals have been scuttled because a seller perceived a slight or an insult by a buyer, or somehow decided the chemistry was just not right.

To many sellers, the sale of the business that he started and devoted much of his life to is a difficult proposition. We've worked with sellers who would almost have less difficulty divorcing their spouses or putting their children up for adoption. Try to be sensitive to this emotional attachment. Don't make the mistake of treating the seller as if he were selling a car, a house, or stock in a public company. While to you each business may be one more situation to check out and evaluate, to a business owner, his business is unique and deserves special consideration and understanding.

An understanding of this emotional attachment is helpful. Few buy/sell deals go through when the buyer and seller feel animosity toward one another. Cooperation and mutual understanding pave the way for a deal far better than do perceived insults and disrespect. You need to understand and be sensitive to the fact that a considerable amount of seller ego is tied up in the business. We have seen several situations where a seller rejects an offer, only to accept a similar or even a less attractive offer from a buyer who he feels would do a better job caring for his business and taking it to the next level.

Mutual Suspicion

If you are considering the purchase of a business, you are well justified in being suspicious of claims, inferences, and anything that just doesn't seem quite right. Your suspicions may include, "What is the seller trying to put over on me? What is he hiding? Does he want to sell because of a potential calamity that I don't know about?" You should also realize that a seller approaches a buyer with apprehensions as well. Typical fears are, "What if this company wants to pump me for information so they can better compete with me or even steal my customers? What if they can't secure the financing? What do they really intend to do with my company if they buy it? What if he takes this business that took me 20 years to build and runs it into the ground?"

There is no easy solution to this mutual suspicion, as it is quite justified, at least initially. In many cases it disappears or is at least lessened after buyer and seller get to know each other. This is why we always try to have the first meeting be a low-pressure, get-to-know one another session. If buyer and seller are not comfortable with one another, the likelihood of a deal is slim.

Buying a business is not like buying a house or a car. After the transaction is completed, the buyer and seller do not just walk away from one another. They usually have to work together for at least a short time and sometimes for an indefinite period of time. For this reason, the chemistry must be reasonably good. If it doesn't start off that way, it is unwise to expect improvement later in the relationship.

Sophisticated buyers and sellers will have their intermediaries "talk tough" and state objections. They reason, "Hey, if this deal goes through, we're going to have to work with each other. Let's not get into arguments and set the stage for a strained relationship." The intermediaries walk away afterwards and don't have to worry about lingering bad feelings, arguments, intransigent positions, objections, or suspicions.

Past Reality Versus Future Potential

Entrepreneurs are noted for their optimism. Sellers are fond of telling buyers what they themselves are convinced of: "The future of this business is so bright that an analysis of past performance can't do it justice." Nevertheless, a buyer needs to gently convince the seller that those past financial statements are an important element of establishing a company's market value.

No One Else Can Run this Business

It is a common attitude among business owners that no one can run their companies as well as they can. It is also common for strategic buyers to look at a business and decide that they can easily do better, which may be an accurate assessment. A seller will typically assume that you will need months of training in the business before you can competently run it. You, on the other hand, may look at the business and figure that with the resources your company will bring to bear you can manage and grow it faster than the current owner can. Obviously, communicating this conclusion to a seller would be highly insulting.

One of the authors was once representing a catalog retailer for sale. The company's founder was absolutely convinced that only she could run the company and freely shared that opinion with prospective buyers. He scheduled a meeting with three executives from a large catalog company that had an aggressive growth by acquisition strategy and that he knew was a very good prospect. Before the meeting he pulled the seller aside and explained that it would not be good to stress her belief that only she could possibly run this company. The prospective buyer, he explained, would only become the actual buyer if they believe that they could run the company. She indicated she understood.

Despite the advice, during the meeting she insisted several times that no one could possibly run this company other than her, noting that her 25 years of knowledge were essential to its operation and survival. He thought the deal was surely slipping away. After nearly an hour the seller was called away. As soon as she was well out of earshot one of the executives said to the others "Well, I don't see anything here that we can't do better, do you guys?" They both shook their head no. These were sophisticated executives who were adept at acquisition. As such, they saw right through the seller's ego based belief that only she could run the company, and of course didn't challenge that belief with the seller.

Incidentally, that company did acquire the seller's business, grew it based on synergistic advantages and resold it three years later at a $2,500,000 profit (with a calculated 36% internal rate of return).

Concern for Employees

Small company owners often have close relationships with their employees. There is a range of relationships to be sure, but some business owners are very protective of their employees and very concerned that they are taken care of in an acquisition. Corporate buyers often reason that they can integrate some of the selling company's operations into the buying company's operations, thereby eliminating employees and saving money. This is a viable cost cutting strategy. However, the seller may not see it as such a great idea. We have seen sellers insist that their employees' jobs be protected for a period of time after the acquisition.

Concern for Customers

A smart entrepreneur knows that his customers are what built his business. As with employees, some business owners insist that their customers or clients receive the same level of service that they are accustomed to going forward and will try to gauge a buyer's ability and intent to treat customers well.

Owner's Role and Status Going Forward

Recently, we arranged the acquisition of a medical services company. The buyer made a very attractive offer. However, one of the two owners (we'll call him Jim) of the selling company balked at the offer and we couldn't understand why. The other partner helped us figure it out. Although Jim would get a good deal of cash from the deal and a nice employment contract, he felt he would lose his status and identity in the community. He would no longer be the part owner of this high profile successful company, but a mere employee of the company he founded. We discussed it with our client, who agreed to give Jim the title of Senior Vice President, as well as a luxury car for full time use. That sealed the deal for Jim.

Will the Seller Really Sell?

Here's a situation you want to avoid:

You find a promising acquisition target. You spend time with the sellers and with the business and decide it merits serious consideration. So you go through their financial and other information more carefully and share your analysis with your internal people and outside advisors. You decide to present a non-binding proposal. After some tweaks and negotiations, you shake hands with the sellers and talk about formalizing the details and moving toward a close in a few months.

A few days later, you get a phone call from the seller saying, "I changed my mind." You get some explanation, which probably doesn't make much sense to you, but it doesn't matter: the seller pulled out of the deal and there is little you can do about it. Perhaps he just changed his mind when the reality of selling the business he worked so hard to start and grow hit him. Perhaps one partner was always lukewarm about the deal while the other was gung-ho. Perhaps his wife or father-in-law or friend or lawyer told him he's crazy to sell, or perhaps he was just fishing in the first place to see what might happen if he offered his business for sale. Again, it doesn't matter: there is little you can do about it.

The best protection against this kind or disappointment is to look for clues as to whether a seller is really likely to consummate a deal. We've been assisting buyers and sellers for many years, and we very much appreciate the danger of a seller not going through with a deal. We spend a good deal of effort trying to make this determination, yet we have no magic formula.

We carefully evaluate everyone's overall enthusiasm for making a deal. If there are multiple owners in your target business, watch carefully to try to determine if they are all on the same page. It is not unusual for one partner to be more enthusiastic about selling than the other(s). So, more likely than not, the one who most wants to sell will be the *point man*—the one who deals with you regarding the possible sale. But the fact that you deal more with one particular partner doesn't mean that he or she has more say over the decision. See Chapter VIII for some tips on dealing with multiple owners.

One of our favorite questions to ask in determining if a seller will really sell is, "What do you want to do once the sale is accomplished?". A crisp answer with clear plans is a good indication that he or she will go through with a sale while an uncertain or nebulous answer is a warning sign.

The crisp, clear answer could be something along the lines of work for the new owner full-time or part-time. Or a better answer still is, "I want to maintain a percentage of the company and work with the new owner to grow the business." Another good answer would be one that involves realizing a long-term non-business goal like, "I plan to move to the beach house we bought in Hawaii five years ago and fully restore it." Reasons to sell that are positive (getting to do what he really wants to do) as opposed to negative (I'm sick of this) are better signs that the seller really is a seller. But any clear plan is better than a vague answer of "I dunno," "we'll see" or "I haven't really thought about it".

Warning Signs

Here are a couple warning signs that the seller may not consummate a deal:

Others Are Driving the Decision to Consider Selling

An owner who is enthusiastically interested in selling is clearly a better candidate than one who is being pressured to do so. If an owner is most interested in selling because his spouse or business partner or someone else is pressuring him to do so, be careful. This seller may well go back to that spouse or partner with lots of reasons why the deal (any deal) is a bad one. Be especially careful if one partner seems to be enthusiastic and the other(s) seem lukewarm or even hostile to a sale.

Past Attempts to Sell (Indecisiveness)

We always ask a prospective seller if he has tried to sell his company before. If the answer is yes, we of course follow up with, "What happened?" If the deal fell through for reasons out of the seller's control, like buyer couldn't get financing, that's not a serious negative. But if it's an answer that indicates the seller backed out or put up unreasonable obstacles ("they low-balled me" or "I just had a bad feeling" or "I got tired of them asking for all kinds of documents"), be very careful. This is a sign of a non-seller, or at least an indecisive one.

One's Whole Identity is His Business

This phenomenon is tougher to spot, but worth looking for. An owner whose whole identity is his business may have difficulty pulling the trigger. Try to get a handle on the owner's life outside his company. Does he talk about his family, travel, hobbies, volunteer activities, even other business interests, or anything else that gives him an identity outside his business? If the answer is no, he may have difficulty letting go of his company because he is his company.

It is certainly not unusual for an owner to show some signs of anxiety in turning over his company to someone else. It is at the very least the closing of a chapter in his life. Owners who are spending more time anticipating the next chapter than mourning the chapter that is closing are much better prospects to go through with actually consummating the sale of their company.

We believe from experience that deals happen when both seller and buyer are motivated to make them happen. If both sides aren't working enthusiastically toward consummating the deal, there likely will be no deal. If a seller is responding quickly to questions and information requests, it is a good sign he is motivated. If, on the other hand, you need to coax the seller along at every step or if he seems to be giving work towards the sale a low priority, that would be a bad sign.

Assessing a seller's willingness to sell is complicated by the fact that even a motivated seller has an incentive to appear somewhat equivocal. If the seller looks too eager, he knows that it may arouse suspicions about whether he believes that the business is going to do well in the future. A buyer may also feel that displaying some ambivalence about selling will help him secure a better price for his company.

Sellers with Inflated Concept of Valuation

As we've stated repeatedly, buying a business is an investment. The same principles that apply to other investment decisions apply. The bigger the perceived risk, the bigger return an investor will demand, should the investment work as planned. The value of a stock, a bond, or a CD follows this principle, as should the value of a business, and to most buyers, it does.

However, many sellers are more than willing to suspend their understanding of financial logic when it comes to selling their business. Business owners, even those with a full understanding of the risk/return principles of investment, somehow think those rules are suspended when it comes to their business. We've heard many explanations, some from sophisticated business people, as to why the basic rules of ROI just don't apply to their particular situation. We've also heard all too often that the rules do apply, but the ROI needs to be computed based on in-house projections as to where the business will be in two, three, or four years. For example: "Yes, 3.5 times EBITDA sounds about right. EBITDA now is about $100,000. However, according to my projections, in three years it will be $250,000. So 250,000 times 3.5 equals $875,000, so I expect to get at least $875,000 for my business."

Unfortunately, there are many intermediaries who are more than willing to take advantage of this *rules of ROI don't apply to my situation* phenomenon. They will tell prospective sellers what they want to hear: "Your business is worth much more than those silly ROI formulas indicate." They will offer some kind of flimsy logic that many sellers are all too eager to accept. It's easy to convince new parents that their baby is intellectually or athletically gifted and it's easy to convince a novice business seller that his business is worth a lot more than it's really worth.

It should be noted that for acquisitions that involve demonstrable synergies or significant economy of scale opportunities, a premium price may well be justified. But that premium is typically in the range of 5% to 25%, and the rules of ROI still apply. It's just that those synergies can enhance the ROI to the buying company in a well-executed strategic acquisition. The problems come in when a seller or an intermediary first defines huge and unattainable strategic gains for the buying company and tries for valuations that are double or triple what a recognized valuation formula would indicate.

Bottom line: you have to define the benefits and value of your company, and internally estimate the ROI based on the price expectations of the seller. If the price is within range based on your internal calculations, keep the negotiations going. Otherwise, politely inform the seller that the acquisition just doesn't work for you based on the asking price.

Beware Seminar Sellers

Unfortunately, a number of companies have taken advantage of this suspension of logic phenomenon in a very big way. They run seminars around the country for business owners who might consider selling. The seminars tend to be very slick and very good at convincing would-be sellers that what they want to believe is true: their business is worth more than financial logic says it's worth. They talk about *hidden assets*, like the name of the company and products or services imagined but not developed. The word *potential* is liberally sprinkled throughout the presentation. They talk about synergies with companies that only they can uncover, and about buyers, typically in Asia or in Mideast oil kingdoms, who will pay two, three, or four times what those *traditional* formulas would indicate.

The rest of the pitch is that you have to pay them an upfront fee of $40,000 or more before they'll perform their magic. The fee, they explain, is to prove you are serious about selling, for the preparation of marketing materials, and for the time and effort needed to learn the business and uncover the hidden value that they can then extract from a buyer. Now, there are a lot of business owners who buy the pitch hook, line and sinker, but stop short of paying the fee, just as there are lots of parents who are easily convinced their two-year-old is destined for Harvard, but might balk at paying $50,000 to someone who says he can get him admitted there when the time comes.

If you are talking with a seller who has seemingly inflated ideas about the value of his company, ask him for the basis of his valuation. If the answer is from a seminar on selling a business, or if he talks about hidden assets or overly generous oil kingdom buyers, and he seems

convinced of this logic, you should walk away. Maybe try again in a few months when his expectations have been tempered by the realities of the marketplace.

VII. Valuing a Company for Acquisitions

There are many reasons to value a company, such as for divorce, estate planning, to value shares bought by an ESOP, or for financial planning. There are also many methods of business valuation, and they are covered in depth in many books, including several by the authors of this book. We will cover only those methods that are appropriate for determining what to pay for an acquisition target. We will also explain the non-financial considerations that are important in determining what price to pay.

Capitalized Earnings Approach

A common method of valuing a business is called the Capitalization of Earnings, or Capitalized Earnings, method. Capitalization refers to the return on investment that is expected by an investor. There are many variations of how this method is applied. However, the basic logic is the same.

To demonstrate the logic of this approach, suppose you had $10,000 to invest. You might look at different stocks, bonds, or savings accounts. You would compare the potential return against the risk of each and make a judgment as to which is the best deal in your particular situation. The same return on investment logic holds for buying a business. Capitalization methods for valuing a business are based upon the return on your investment as the new owner.

To further demonstrate the capitalization method of valuation, pretend that you are considering the purchase of a highly oversimplified business. Pretend the business is simply a post office box to which people send money. The magic post office box has been collecting money at the rate of about $10,100 per year steadily for ten years with very little variation. It is likely to continue to collect money at this rate indefinitely. The only expense for this business is $100 per year rent charged by the post office for the box. So the business earns $10,000 per year ($10,100-$100). Because the box will continue to collect money indefinitely at the same rate, it retains its full value. You should be able to sell it at any time and get back your initial investment.

You would probably look at this "no risk" business earning $10,000 and compare it to other ways of investing your money to earn $10,000 per year. A near no-risk investment like a savings account or government treasury bills might pay about 4% a year. At the 4% rate, for someone to earn the same $10,000 per year that the magic PO box earns, an investment of $250,000 (250,000 x 4%= $10,000) would be required. Therefore, the PO box's value is in the area of $250,000. It is an equivalent investment in terms of risk and return to the savings account or T-bill.

Now, the real world of small business has no magic PO boxes and no "no risk" situations. Business owners take risks, have expenses, and business equipment can and usually does depreciate in value. The higher that you believe the risk to be, the higher the capitalization rate (percentage) you should use to estimate value. Rates of 25% to 40% are common for small business capitalization calculations. That is, a return on your investment of 25% to 40% is appropriate in buying a small business. Finally, it is important to point out that the return on investment should be in addition to a fair salary for yourself or for a manager whom you will hire.

Excess Earnings Method

The Excess Earnings method (also called the Capitalization of Excess Earnings or CEE method) is the best valuation method for a wide range of small businesses. The basis of the method is quite simple. It states that the value of a business is equal to the tangible net worth plus goodwill.

VALUE = NET WORTH + GOODWILL

The goodwill, in turn, is equal to a multiplier, which will be explained below, times the annual excess earnings. Again, earnings in this context exclude a reasonable salary to the owner.

GOODWILL = MULTIPLIER x EXCESS EARNINGS

Finally, excess earnings are defined as the EBITDA (Earnings before interest, taxes, depreciation, and amortization) of the business minus a reasonable carrying cost for the money that must be invested in the fixed assets of the business.

Excess Earnings = EBITDA − (Value of Assets X Financing Rate of Assets

In simple terms, this means the value of a business is equal to the net worth— the inventory, accounts receivable, etc.— plus a certain number of years of profit. That number, or multiplier is typically somewhere between 1 and 6. In the section below, "The Earnings Multiplier," we will discuss how to arrive at an appropriate multiplier. For the time being, let's assume the multiplier is 3.This means a business with a multiplier of 3 is valued at the net worth plus a three-year sum of excess earnings.

So a business with $300,000 of tangible net worth, excess earnings of

$200,000, and a multiplier of 3 would be worth:

GOODWILL = MULTIPLIER x EXCESS EARNINGS

VALUE = NET WORTH + GOODWILL

GOODWILL = 3 x $200,000 = $600,000

VALUE = $300,000 + $600,000 = $900,000

In the real world, it is not quite so simple. The financial statements provided by the seller usually need some recasting before computing an appropriate value for the company. To illustrate this, let's pretend that you are considering the purchase of two companies. Both companies are roughly the same size in terms of gross revenues and in terms of unadjusted earnings. However, they are actually very different in terms of their adjusted earnings and in their financial requirements.

Items that commonly need to be adjusted to properly value the business are the following:

Owner's compensation: The owners' wages and benefits are usually included in the financial statements. The owners, however, are often not paid at a fair market rate. As a buyer you will either retain the owner(s) at a fair salary or hire replacements. You must adjust the owner's compensation and benefits to the true cost of replacing the owner(s).

Related party transactions: Often, the owner(s) will have transactions with related entities at non-market rates. For example, the owner(s) and their families frequently hold real estate in a separate LLC, which rents the real estate to the business. Those facilities might be rented by the business at a non-market rate. The rent needs to reflect what you will pay on the open market, not the non-market rate rent.

Adjusting book value to fair market value. The fair market value of equipment needs to be determined if it is a material amount. Equipment and buildings are usually depreciated or expensed as quickly as possible to reduce taxes.

Interest: The amount of interest that a business pays depends on the capital structure of the business. Since after the acquisition you will have a different capital structure, interest expenses are not included in the EBITDA calculation

Depreciation and Amortization: When valuing a business, depreciation and amortization are often eliminated, since these expenses are non-cash expenses that are in large part determined by choice of accounting methods. However, in a capital-intensive business these expenses may be both material and real. For example, we assisted a non-emergency medical transportation company in making acquisitions, and they did not exclude depreciation in calculating the valuation, since the vehicle fleet depreciation was a real expense. It is important, however, when comparing companies to make sure that you use the same method of calculating depreciation.

The Earnings Multiplier

There are a number of factors that will have impact upon the future of a business. The factors that are generally considered for valuation purposes are competitiveness, the industry as a whole, risk, the performance of the firm being valued relative to the industry, industry and company growth projections, location, and the desirability or appeal of the business. Each of these factors is rated on a scale of 1 to 6. A higher number means a better rating, with 6 as the best and 1 as the worst. Ratings are based largely upon subjective judgment, upon industry projections, and upon industry performance statistics. All the items used in setting the multiplier are assigned a number separately; then all the numbers are averaged.

A warning here is that there is nothing cast in stone regarding the multiplier. Different people will have different opinions, not only about items like desirability, but also about the interpretation of projections, competitive strengths, and so on. Nevertheless, using a system like this to determine the multiplier does make the valuation process more objective, and provides some criteria based rationale for setting a value and ultimately for defending the reasonableness of an offering price.

We have developed an online business valuation calculator that uses the excess earnings method of valuation. You'll just need to answer some financial and non-financials questions, and the application produces an estimated business valuation. The basic valuation is free and the site allows you to order a low priced downloadable report. www.ezvaluation.com.

Comparison of Excess Earnings and Capitalized Earnings Approach

An observant reader will note that the methods we outlined for determining value thus far are very similar. The Capitalized Earnings approach just looks at the rate of return on your investment, whereas the Excess Earnings approach looks at the balance sheet of the company as well. So, if we have two companies, each of which creates $1,000,000 in EBITDA, but one of which has a more asset heavy balance sheet with the Capitalized Earnings approach, their value would be the same, but using the Excess Earnings methodology the company with the stronger balance sheet would be worth more. The values may be the same for a business if the business valuation is done both ways because the multiples used in the excess earnings are lower.

Often, we hear buyers say that they are not in the business of investing in assets, or that the assets are, in their view, just necessary to create the earnings that they are buying so they are already paying for the assets when they buy the earnings. Considering the balance sheet certainly makes the valuation process more complicated, but we believe that it produces a more accurate valuation. Let's look at why.

Financing Costs and WACC

In the real world, banks (and other sources of financing) are willing to lend far more when loans are backed by assets than when they are backed only by earnings. We recently sold a business for $1.8 Million that had highly variable earnings (EBITDA ranged from $200,000 to $800,000 with a 6 year average of $350,000). The owner had died after a long battle with cancer and the estate wanted the business sold quickly because they were afraid that the highly skilled employees were nervous about their future and would leave the company, draining it of any value. The business buyer financed the deal as follows: $800,000 in a mortgage against the building, $200,000 in bank loan backed by inventory, $250,000 from factoring the receivables, and $350,000 in a seller note. They put some money into the deal, but not a lot. Even after they paid legal and accounting fees, they probably invested less than $300,000, less than an average year's EBITDA. They were able to do so largely because the business was asset-rich. Their average weighted cost of capital was very low because they were able to finance most of the purchase at favorable rates, using the assets as collateral.

Assets Have Value Beyond Financing

You buy a business in the hope that it will be profitable and will grow. However, sometimes businesses fail, often for reasons that you don't or can't foresee. The economy is unpredictable, technologies change, and new competitors emerge. In the event that things change and your purchase is not viable as an ongoing concern having assets to sell off can reduce (or possibly even eliminate) your losses. In the case of a merger, some assets may not be needed after the closing and so can be quickly sold off without impacting operations, essentially reducing the purchase price.

Cost to Create Approach (Leapfrog Start-up)

You may be purchasing a company just to avoid the difficulties of starting from scratch, since a startup takes time and money. Following this line of reasoning, it may be justified to pay a premium of 10% or 15% above the sum of projected startup costs due to the time and effort that you will save.

Usually, a profitable business is worth more than this approach will justify. A business that is not profitable may have flaws that should discourage its purchase. If you bought this kind of business, you would be inheriting those flaws, such as bad location, bad reputation, production problems, etc. Its primary use is in situations where no other method is appropriate, such as a business that was started recently and has not yet had enough time to begin producing profits, or in combination with other methods of valuation.

Rules of Thumb Methods

Many people are convinced that there are some quick rules of thumb that could determine the value of a business. Some of these rules of thumb state, for example, that an insurance agency is worth 1.5 times annual commissions, or that a chemical manufacturing company is worth 6 times its EBIT. These formulas may indeed be fair averages, but they give very little help in determining the value of a particular business.

The main problem with rule of thumb formulas is that they are statistically derived from the sale of many businesses of each type. That is, an organization might compile statistics on perhaps 50 chemical manufacturers that were sold over a three-year period. They will then average all the selling prices and calculate that the average chemical company sold for an amount equivalent to 6 times EBIT. The rule of thumb is thus created. However, some of those companies may have sold for 2 times EBIT, while other for 7 or 8 times EBIT.

Another issue is that to get enough companies to create the rule of thumb an overly broad sample is often used. A rule of thumb for chemical companies may include transactions of chemical companies that sell commodity chemicals, specialty chemicals, and a mix of the two. It may include companies that are urban or rural, that manufacture exclusively domestically, internationally, or both. Perhaps there are significant differences between companies that only manufacture and those that also resell chemicals manufactured by others or between those that sell only wholesale and those that sell retail as well. The rule of thumb assumes a homogeneity in the data set that does not exist.

The business with expenses and profits that are right on target with industry averages may well sell for a price in line with the rule of thumb formula. Others will vary. It is not appropriate to apply the rule of thumb to a business that varies significantly from the average.

Nevertheless, industry averages can be a good quick and dirty starting point to valuation. Check with industry associations for rule of thumb formulas for buying a business.

Rule of thumb approaches tend to work in two situations: One is in industries that are rapidly undergoing consolidation, especially if the rolled up companies are being taken public. In the late 1990s and early 2000s, for example, ISPs were bought and sold based on number of subscribers or subscriber revenues. The other situation in which rules of thumb work well is in acquisitions where the cost structure of the acquired company is almost irrelevant to the acquirer. An example is the payroll industry. When a large payroll processor acquires a small operation, the percentage of revenues spent on labor, software, rent, etc. becomes irrelevant as the customers are switched to the larger processors software and systems.

Value of Specific Intangible Assets

This is an often-overlooked approach to valuation. Yet in some cases, especially companies acquiring other companies, it is the only appropriate approach that will result in a sale. The approach is based upon the buyer's buying a wanted intangible asset versus creating it. Often, buying can be a cost-efficient and time-saving alternative.

For example, we recently sold a temporary employment agency. This agency specialized in matching people with certain computer skills with organizations that temporarily needed those skills. Because there was a shortage of these workers in the area in which the selling company did business, placing workers was not difficult. However, finding qualified workers was very difficult.

We approached firms in the same or related businesses. Through our research, we calculated that recruiting a qualified worker for this industry costs an agency at least $500. Therefore, we asked a price of $450.00 for each worker in the pool of available employees. To the buyer, this acquisition strategy not only saved $50.00 per worker, but it also cut down on the time it took to recruit. The overhead of the selling company was not an issue because the buying company already had the system in place that the overhead expense was paying for (offices, computer system, phones, etc.). In fact, whether the seller was making or losing money was of little consequence to the buyer. The value to the buyer was the value of buying qualified workers versus recruiting qualified workers through the more traditional methods of advertising, interviewing, etc.

A common application of this method in a strategic acquisition is buying a customer base that recurs on a regular and predictable basis. Customers with a high likelihood of being retained barring an extraordinary change (customers that are almost easier to keep than to lose) are valuable in most industries. Examples of industries where companies are bought and sold primarily based upon the value of the recurring customer base with regular and predictable need for service include insurance agencies, payroll services, internet service providers, and internet hosting companies.

If you plan to buy a business primarily for its customer base, insist on a credit for each customer that is not retained for a stated period of time. For example, you may want to offer $200 per customer, but with a pro-rated credit for each customer that is lost during the twelve months following the closing of the sale. Pro-ration is based upon when the customer leaves—if a customer leaves after 6 months, for example, half of the $200 would be returned to you.

The Discounted Cash Flow (DCF) Method

There are situations where the past performance of a company may not be the best predictor of its future performance. If a company's financial performance is likely to change after the sale (in either a positive or negative way) then you should value the company based on the projected future performance. Examples of situations where the DCF method might be appropriate include valuing a company that just gained or lost a major customer; recently made significant investments in sales, manufacturing, or research and development that have not yet created new sales, but which you are confident will result in extraordinary growth; industry changes that either benefit or hurt the company being valued (e.g. the bankruptcy of a competitor, a new technology that reduces costs); or in the special case of a merger or acquisition (which is discussed in detail in Chapter IV).

You may feel that you will be able to manage a company you are buying better than the current owner can manage it. However, this is generally not the kind of situation where relying on the DCF method is appropriate. The improved performance is a result of your effort (and capital investment). Therefore the benefits of your labor, expertise, and investment should accrue to you not to the seller.

DCF - How it Works

The discounted cash flow method allows you to value a business based on projected future cash flows. Of course, money that you expect a business to produce in the future is worth less than money today. There are a number of reasons that this is true: inflation can erode the value of money, there is uncertainty that you will receive money in the future, and money spent today cannot be put to use (either by being invested or by being spent on something to consume).

We have created a calculator that you can use to perform the calculations discussed below. The calculator allows you to assume that you will receive a lump sum at the end (e.g. you plan to sell the business), or that there is a steady income stream for a period of time, a growing income stream for a period of time, or a perpetual stream of income at the end (with or without growth).

If you are using this method to value an acquisition target, you must go through the DCF calculation twice, first for your company without the acquisition and then again for the two companies combined. Once you have done both calculations, subtract the value of your company that was calculated without the acquisition from the value of the combined companies. This difference is the maximum value of the acquisition target to you.

Discount Rate

The most common way to calculate how much future cash flows are worth is to discount the cash flows using a discount rate that is derived by adding two components. The first component is the risk-free rate, which is the rate of return that a buyer could achieve by investing the money in an essentially risk-free investment (in the U.S. a treasury bond with a maturity similar to the time frame being projected is often used). The second component is a discount for risk.

Typical discount rates for risk might be:

- 20-30% for businesses with annual sales over $20,000,000 and some barriers to entry.
- 25-35% for businesses with sales between $10,000,000 and $20,000,000 and some barriers to entry.
- 30-50% for businesses with sales under $10,000,000 and low barriers to entry.
-

There is overlap in the ranges because other factors can increase or decrease the risk premium, including customer concentration, volatility of earnings history, reliance on key employees, and threat of litigation.

Assuming that the acquisition target is smaller or close in size to your company, when doing this calculation for both a combined entity and your business as a stand-alone we suggest that you use a discount rate that is appropriate for the stand-alone entity for both the stand-alone entity and the combined entity, even though the combined entity would, if evaluated by itself, have a lower discount rate. This gives a more conservative valuation and does not inflate the value of the acquisition based solely on its size. If the acquisition target is significantly larger than your company we would advocate using a discount rate that is appropriate for the acquisition target as a stand-alone entity for both your company and the combined entity.

Weighted Average Cost of Capital

An alternative way to determine the discount rate is to use the Weighted Average Cost of Capital. Using this method, you determine the average return demanded for all of the capital used in the business and use that as the discount rate. For example, suppose we have a business that we are buying for $10,000,000 and we are financing as follows:

Amount	Source	Rate
1,000,000	Note from Seller	5%
5,000,000	Bank Loan	9%
4,000,000	Equity Investment	35%

The weighted average cost of capital would be:

10% (percentage financed at Seller Note Rate) times 5% (amount Financed at Seller Note rate)

plus 50% (percentage financed at Bank Loan rate) of the amount financed times 9% (percentage financed at Bank Loan rate)

plus 40% (percentage financed at Equity rate) of the amount financed times 35% (percentage financed at Equity rate)

$0.05 \times 0.1 + 0.09 \times 0.5 + 0.35 \times 0.4 = 19\%$ Weighted Average Cost of Capital

Future Cash Flows

Once a discount rate is determined, future cash flows are projected. The cash flows are generally projected for three to five years in the future. Cash flows after the period that is being forecast are assumed to grow at a terminal rate. The terminal rate is generally far lower than the rate of growth used during the forecast period because as businesses mature they tend to grow more slowly and after the initial period of growth the boost from synergies with an acquiring company and new management has taken place.

Synergies and Economies of Scale

When a business is acquired and merged with another company, the newly combined company may be able to buy materials in bulk and thereby reduce costs. Many functions, such as payroll, accounting, information technology, and facilities management can be consolidated yielding cost savings. In some cases, locations can be closed. Details of how to project sales and expenses after a merger are discussed in more detail in the chapter on buying a competitor.

New Products and Services

If the company being sold has developed or acquired new products that are not yet producing revenue, then an argument can be made that the revenue from those products should be adjusted for. However, in high technology industries such as software a buyer will not accept that argument unless the new technology goes above and beyond the normal R & D needed to stay current and competitive.

New Customers and Contracts

If there are major new customers, especially with signed contracts, that will materially change the financial performance of the company that can be a reason to base the sale on future projections instead of past performance.

Increased Investment

If the company being acquired has made major investments that will improve its financial performance, then future cash flow projections should be used. For example, if new machinery has just been installed that will allow a manufacturer to make twice as many widgets an hour, the widget manufacturer can argue that future cash flows will be far higher than past cash flows. Buyers will sometimes counter that argument with the argument that becoming more productive is a normal part of doing business. All widget manufacturers are becoming more productive, they will claim, and prices will fall as a result of the industry's increased productivity. Be prepared to demonstrate that your investment really is extraordinary and will pay off with increased cash flows if you are arguing that you deserve to be paid for a past investment.

Adjusting Future Cash Flows to Present Value

Once you have forecast future cash flows you discount them back to what they are worth today using the following formula:

For each period (usually we use annual numbers)

$PV = FV/(1+r)n$
Where PV is the present value, FV is the future value, r is the discount rate, and n is the number of periods.

Terminal Value

After the last period that has been forecasted, we need the value of the enterprise. Some buyers, such as private equity groups that plan to flip the company in three to five years, may forecast a terminal value (what they think they will be able to sell the company for at that point), but we prefer to assume that the business will then become a perpetuity (or a growing perpetuity where growth is assumed to approximate the historical growth rate of the industry)

For the final value, the perpetuity that we assume at the end the formula changes a bit to

$$PV = (PP/r)/(1+r)n$$

Where PP is the perpetuity payment.

Or if the perpetuity is growing we can include the growth rate by adjusting the formula as follows:

$$PV = (PP/r-g)/(1+r)n$$

Where g is the growth rate of the perpetuity.

It is easy to be overly optimistic about the terminal growth rate, but most businesses do not grow faster than the economy as a whole, since the economy's growth rate is just the growth rate of all of the businesses that make up that economy. Furthermore, mature, established businesses tend to grow more slowly than the average business. Be very cautious when forecasting a growth rate because a small change in growth rate assumption can produce a surprisingly large change in value because growth compounds and a perpetuity lasts forever.

Once again, we recommend that you hire a third party valuation professional to help in using the discounted cash flow valuation method. The calculations are a bit technical and can be complicated to the uninitiated. More than that, an outside person is less likely to underestimate the risks involved, than is a buyer with his heart set on taking over the business at hand. You can contact us for assistance, using the contact information at the end of the book.

DCF Example

Let's look at a simplified example of how DCF works. Suppose you buy a company with constant annual sales of $1,000,000 and cash expenses of $500,000. Two years after closing, you plan to add a second factory at a cost of $2,000,000, which will double annual sales and increase cash expenses by $300,000. You believe that you will be able to sell the company for $6,500,000 after five years. You choose a discount rate for this venture of 30%. Here is what the DCF calculation will look like:

Year (n)	1	2	3	4	5
Initial Purchase					
Sales	1,000,000	1,000,000	2,000,000	2,000,000	2,000,000
Expenses	500,000	500,000	800,000	800,000	800,000
CapEx		- 2,000,000			
Sale of Company					6,500,000
Cash Flow	1,500,000	-500,000	2,800,000	2,800,000	9,300,000
$1/(1+r)^n$	0.76923	0.59171	0.45516	0.35012	0.26932
Value of discounted cash flows	1,153,846	(295,858)	1,274,465	980,358	2,504,760
Total Discounted value	5,617,572				

We get a Discounted value of $5,617,572 based on the cash flows projected. You'll notice that we only considered cash expenses for this analysis. Hence, the entire $2,000,000 for the new factory was shown as an expense in the year that the factory was built. No depreciation expenses are included. Of course, taxes are a cash flow item and a reduction based on depreciation of the new factory is incorporated into the expenses line in our example.

Comparison to Public Company Multiples

One way to value a company is to compare it to similar companies that are publicly traded. While it is appealing for a seller to do so, the comparison is hard to make. There are several things that a seller typically ignores or underestimates when using this method. As a buyer, you need to be ready to deal with this all-too-common wishful thinking on the part of sellers.

A publicly traded stock is very liquid, such that you can sell it in minutes. Even thinly traded small capitalization stocks will be bought by a market maker if no other buyers are available. The business you are buying, however, is highly illiquid and can take many months or years to sell. Hence, publicly traded companies have a liquidity premium built into their price.

Generally, there is a great deal more information publicly available about any listed company than there is about the company that you are buying. There are rules designed to limit the ability of insiders to take advantage of their superior knowledge about the company. In a private transaction, there is a discount for the information asymmetry between you and the buyer, because no matter how well you study the transaction, you will not understand the company and its prospects as well as the seller does.

Public companies incur compliance costs that are not incurred by privately held companies. These costs are already reflected in the financial statements of the public companies. Should a seller want to compare his company to a publicly traded one, it would be reasonable to ask that he first recast his financial statements to account for listing and compliance costs.

Finally, when sellers compare their company to publicly listed companies, they often just use the P/E ratio provided by a broker or website. These P/E ratios, however, treat interest, depreciation, amortization, and taxes as expenses. They then compare the P/E ratio to the multiple that you are applying to EBITDA, which does not include the interest, depreciation, amortization, and tax expenses.

Smaller Companies Carry More Risk

Smaller companies are also inherently more risky, for a variety of reasons. In general, smaller companies tend to be less well capitalized, have less access to capital markets and other sources of financing, have less pricing power, have fewer customers across which they can spread expenses such as G&A or R&D, and so on. Smaller companies are also at greater risk from external events. For example, a competitor that opens nearby will more significantly impact a retailer with a single location than a chain with fifty locations.

Roll Ups

One strategy that Private Equity Groups and others often use is to buy a number of smaller companies, consolidate them, and sell the combined entity in an IPO at a public company multiple. One of the authors was approached by a group offering such a consolidation deal during the Internet boom in the late 1990s. The deal offered did not even require a complete sale of the company, allowing those selling their companies to participate in the gain as the multiple went up. Although the author did not participate, the strategy was successful.

Summary

There is no perfect way to value a company for buying and selling purposes. Ultimately, the value of a company is the perceived value to a buyer who is ready, willing, and able to buy it. In the case of a strategic acquisition, the purchasing company needs to do an internal valuation to determine the target's worth to that company and the degree to which the target meets the buyer's acquisition goals. However, there are a number of approaches to estimating value, some of which are discussed above. For most privately held smaller companies, the excess earnings approach is generally the preferred method of valuation. When making an offer, it can be helpful to demonstrate the reasonableness of that offer based upon a recognized valuation method.

Evaluating an Acquisition Beyond the Financial Statements

Much of what you need to know to make a decision on purchasing a business is contained in its current and past financial statements. However, financial statements do not tell the entire story. There are several things to watch for and to examine that are either not part of a financial statement, or are at best merely suggested by those statements. Financial statements tell much about a firm's past, but you are really interested in its future.

Accountants and other financial professionals will warn you not to consider purchasing a company without closely analyzing its financial statements. We would not disagree with this advice. However, we will add that it is equally as foolish to rely solely on a company's financial statements to make a buy/no buy decision. Before buying, there is more you need to know about than a company's past financial performance. Some of the recommended non-financial evaluation steps are outlined in this section.

Order Pipeline

Many businesses have a long lead-time for sales. For example, we currently have a listing for a business that fabricates and erects large steel tanks that store oil, chemicals, bio-fuels, asphalt, and even water. This company typically submits a bid proposal over a year before they do the work. After the bid is accepted and a contract is signed, it can still be many months before work on the project begins. Recently, the company received a signed contract that brought their backlog of signed orders from $15 million to $19 million. Clearly, the business is more attractive with the additional signed contract.

When evaluating a business that has an order pipeline like the one discussed above, it is important to understand how the work backlog compares to historical norms, the chances of bids turning into jobs, the details (and hence the future profit margins) of work in the pipeline, and the capital requirements you will need to address in order to complete the work.

Recurring Revenues

Some businesses have steady recurring revenue streams. For example, a janitorial company may have customers with annual contracts that are provided with services that are billed weekly.

Other businesses, such as retail establishments, typically don't have recurring revenue; every sale is a one-time event. Of course, there are businesses with both recurring and episodic revenue streams, such as a software company that has both initial sales (including installation services) and software maintenance fees.

Recurring revenues are generally worth more than the equivalent amount of episodic revenue, because the cash flow is steadier and more predictable. When evaluating a business, make sure you understand the proportion of revenues that are recurring, the duration of outstanding contracts, the typical contract renewal rates, and any problems with existing contract customers.

Off Balance Sheet and Contingent Liabilities

Sometimes businesses have contingent liabilities that are not shown on the balance sheet. For example, some businesses provide warrantees on their products, but do not create a reserve against future warrantee claims. While these may not be large expenses if there are new products or changes in production techniques, before the closing you can find that you have acquired a liability that you did not expect.

In some cases, the contingent liabilities are large enough that they should be footnoted by the accounting firm, but sometimes they just go unrecognized. In a recent sale in which we were involved, the company's unionized employees were part of a multi-employer pension plan. During due diligence we found that the pension plan was underfunded and that the current withdrawal liability was

$4,000,000, a very significant percentage of the contemplated $10,000,000 sale price. The seller argued that because they did not plan to withdrawal from the pension plan and that the markets could bounce back and wipeout the funding deficit, the liability was not real. Ultimately, a compromise was reached that involved a contingent note.

Management Team

Unless the company that you are acquiring is very small, it likely has a management team in place. You need to evaluate that team to see how well their skills match the needs of your organization, how likely the team is to remain in the intermediate and long term, how easy it will be to learn their skill sets if they do leave, and how easy it will be to work with the acquired company's personnel. You need to understand any non-compete and confidentiality agreements that the management team has with their employer, and whether you can enforce those agreements after a sale.

A successful acquisition can be used to round out your management team. If you have weak financial management, but strong sales, a company that has a great finance team brings more to the table, from your perspective, than one with strong marketing management.

Management Systems

Some businesses have invested heavily in management systems. These systems can include formal documentation of processes, workflow management tools, ERP software, supply chain management systems and more. These systems can include formal registration (such as ISO:9000 or QS9000).

Many formal management systems include well-documented procedures, continuous quality improvement, measurement of customer and employee satisfaction, and a methodology for solving novel problems and making sure that they do not reoccur.

Buying a business with a formalized management system can help with the transition and enable you to detect problems earlier than you would notice them in the absence of such a system. Quality management systems can also confer a competitive advantage in marketing and sales.

Corporate Culture

Your business has a culture that works for you. Corporate culture has so many facets that it is hard to define, but the closer the cultures are, the easier it will be to integrate your businesses. There are many obvious facets of corporate culture – is the dress code casual or suit and tie? Are workers competitive or collegial? Are work hours fixed or flexible? However, there are deeper levels of corporate culture, which are based on how management interacts with workers.

Take as an example a software business that we once sold. This business had a formal management system such that procedures were well documented, and a highly automated workflow management system, which helped ease the transition to new management.

The new owners, however, made several changes. The seller had maintained an open book policy: every employee received a complete set of financial statements every month, a policy that made the new owners uncomfortable, perhaps in part because they assumed a heavy debt load to finance the transition. The financial transparency under the old owners allowed compensation to be based largely on bonuses determined by profitability. The new managers of the software business decided to scrap the open book policy and reduce the importance of bonuses in the compensation scheme. In theory, the workers who now received larger base salaries should have been happy to have a more predictable income stream. However, the open book policy and the opportunity to share in gains when results improved were part of the atmosphere that attracted these particular highly skilled workers to the company. The changes resulted in a slow exodus of the workers to other companies, reducing the value of the company to the acquirer.

When you assess a company, pay careful attention to the culture, the atmosphere, and the personnel policies, and carefully evaluate how much that will change under your management. The greater the changes, the more chance you have for some workers to become disaffected. In a scenario in which much of the value of the business depends on your ability to retain skilled workers, you need to be certain that the transition will be not change the culture in a way that will alienate them.

Cash Off the Top

In the case of very small retail businesses, some owners will maintain that they earn a lot more than is being reported to the government. No doubt this is often true. The question is, should you as a buyer pay a premium for cash coming off the top, based on the owner's say so? In general, the answer is no. In all cases if a buyer is making claims of cash off the top, proceed with extreme caution. Some will counsel that if a seller is cheating the government, he is probably cheating you too. While this argument is a bit simplistic, the point is a valid one.

Some buyers who are sophisticated in buying cash businesses use a number of analytical techniques to estimate just how much is coming off the top. For example, experienced trucking company buyers will look closely at fuel bills to determine approximate sales volume estimates from that information. Buyers of retail stores will look at the store's prices and wholesale costs, and then look at the gross sales and cost of goods sold figures on the firm's tax return. If, for example, you know a store's markup policy and its cost of goods sold, you can estimate true sales and profit figures from those numbers. If a store consistently sets price by doubling the amount it pays for each item, the gross sales figure should be close to double the cost of goods sold, or there should be a viable and documented explanation as to why it is not. In any case, if you are considering the purchase of a cash business, it is a good idea to work the business, actually staying on the premises all day, posing as an employee, for a week or two weeks to get a hands-on measure of actual sales volume. It is never advisable to take a seller's word for it if he or she claims cash is coming off the top. Such a claim is at least a clue to the owner's character, and should signal caution. We have seen businesses with tax returns indicating net income well under $70,000, while their owners tell us they are really earning mid-six figure incomes on a regular basis. Our reaction to outlandish claims such as these has been to not get involved. First of all, we don't want to be in the position of helping to convince a buyer that this is a profitable business when we don't know that to be the case. Secondly, we are immediately suspicious of a seller who is claiming to cheat the government on such a grandiose scale, and we prefer not to do business with people who we don't trust. Finally, we are afraid that if the claims are true, and if the owner is routinely so willing to tell people, the IRS may come in at any time and close down the operation.

New and Pending Legislation

When we were new to business brokerage, we listed a medical temporary employment service. The business recruited nurses and nurses' aids, and offered their services to hospitals and other health care facilities. The financial statements were picture perfect—a solid upward trend, with current owner compensation (profit and salary) approaching $500,000 per year. The statements were CPA audited, leaving little doubt as to their accuracy. We thought that at the asking price of $1,000,000, this would be an easy sale. We first presented the business to a larger company in a neighboring state. The vice president looked at the financials and was impressed. He then asked about pending state legislation regarding nurse temporary agencies. He went on to explain that in Massachusetts, where his company was located, recent legislation severely cut into profits of most agencies. We went back and looked into pending legislation and found that sure enough, there was a bill before the legislature modeled after the Massachusetts bill. Furthermore, we talked to people in the business and were told that either the pending bill or one like it was expected to pass within months. We now knew that this million-dollar listing was overpriced based on this new information.

Now we know enough to check on possible legislative and legal changes that can affect a business before offering it for sale. You should be aware of legal situations that can be expected to impact a business before making an offer to purchase. Ask the owner, others in the industry, industry associations, your state legislator(s), or your lawyer. This kind of eventuality will not show up on a financial statement, no matter how carefully it is scrutinized. A seller or his representative may not know about or may be purposely not mentioning it—it is up to you to find out.

Don't overlook the fact that legal changes can work both ways. That is, they can have a positive effect on some types of companies. For example, a large conglomerate recently purchased a medium size firm that manufactures insulated electrical cable. The target firm was surviving, but struggling. The type of insulation used for its cabling did not meet electrical code in many areas, making sales impossible, except in those few areas that accepted this kind of insulation.

However, the large company knew that another firm that manufactured the same kind of cable was engaged in an all-out campaign to convince local authorities that this cabling was absolutely safe. This campaign was met with a lot of success. The acquiring company reasoned that it could acquire the target firm, and reap the benefits of the campaign that its competitor was paying for. The campaign to change electrical code would expand the market for all players, not just the campaign's sponsor. The point is to be aware of legislative and related issues that can have a powerful impact on a business. Laws and legislation can and do ruin businesses and propel others from mediocrity to success. Such changes can dwarf the relevance of historical financial data.

New Competition

In our free market system, competition is a fact of life. It is a normal part of the business environment. However, there are situations in which changes in the competitive environment can have an unusually severe impact on a business. We once received a call from the owner of a very successful natural food store. He asked if we could meet to discuss the sale of his store. This surprised us because we spoke with him a few months earlier, and he had expressed no interest in selling. At the meeting, he told us that business was going well, and the new health awareness could only help his business. We asked him why he changed his mind and wanted to sell now. He offered only a vague response.

After our meeting we asked friends who were natural food enthusiasts if they had heard any news about natural food marketing in this area. One person said, "Sure, haven't you heard? A supermarket-size natural food store is opening in town." When we asked where it would be located, we knew that we had found the answer. The new store was to open about a half mile from the store that was looking to sell. Had a buyer bought this heretofore successful natural food store based upon past financial performance, that buyer would have been in for an unpleasant surprise. This new competitor was more robust than the kind of competition that most small retailers are able to face successfully. This natural foods supermarket was a huge store with big dollars for advertising, lower prices due to massive buying power, and a stellar reputation both as a champion of the cause of natural food, and as a successful business.

Within eight months of our meeting, the owner who was looking to sell filed for bankruptcy. The new natural food supermarket had quite literally put him out of business.

Competition, the Long View

In evaluating competition, it is important to avoid taking too narrow a view. You should look not only at direct competitors, but also at indirect competitors. For example, a video producer may consider only other video producers to be competition, while a toy store owner may consider only other toy stores as competitors. This view of competition is too narrow because it defines competition from the perspective of the business. Competition should be defined from the perspective of the customer. For example, suppose you are an aunt or uncle taking care of your six-year-old nephew for a Saturday afternoon. You have budgeted fifty dollars to spend for entertaining your six-year-old charge. You offer him several recreational choices such as a movie, roller-skating, an amusement park, a museum, or a visit to a toy store with a purchase of up to the fifty dollar limit. From your perspective (or more to the point, from your nephew's perspective) the movie, roller-skating rink, amusement park, and museum are all competitors of the toy store for your dollars. As a prospective business buyer, being aware of the competition in a broader sense will lead to a more far-reaching pre-purchase evaluation.

As another example, recall the temporary medical employment agency discussed above (in the New and Pending Legislation subsection). That company offers workers the flexibility of working only when they want to work. This policy helps them attract qualified workers because it is a real advantage since health care facilities typically have rotating shifts that require full time and some weekend hours. Now this agency is losing its advantage because the health care facilities, tired of paying premium prices for staff from temporary agencies, are in effect setting up their own in-house agencies. That is, workers can apply to work through the in-house pool, meaning the facility offers no guarantee of work on any day, nor do the workers guarantee availability. This flexible staffing model is essentially the same arrangement as that offered by the agency. It comprises competition from a new and heretofore unexpected source—the customer. Only a prospective buyer taking the long view of competition could have anticipated this source of competition.

Outdated Facilities

Be careful about buying a business that has production equipment that is inefficient by modern standards. If another company has equipment that will do the job better and/or cheaper, the firm with the outdated equipment may eventually find itself at a competitive disadvantage, resulting in a gradual atrophy of business. It can also be dangerous if your equipment is dated even if the competition has equally dated equipment. The competition may upgrade, forcing you to do the same or lose business. Or, a new competitor may emerge, reasoning that an opportunity exists because others in the industry are using dated and inefficient equipment.

We are not implying that a company must buy every new piece of equipment that shows up on the market. That equipment only has an economic justification if it will lead to better product, lower cost, or new business. Buying new equipment without economic justification is no slower a route to business problems than is operating with outdated facilities.

Location

The location of a business is vitally important. Unless you are acquiring the business as a way of expanding your territory geographically, you need to carefully consider travel time, expense, and the difficulty of managing remote location(s). You may want to reassign an existing executive to participate in the management of the acquired company.

You need to consider the attributes of the area in which the business is located. Is there well-developed infrastructure, a pool of potential employees? What is the proximity to customers? Generally, businesses in rural, remote, and inaccessible locations are less attractive and sell for lower multiples.

Economic Sensitivities

Some businesses are relatively immune to cyclical economic changes. A pharmacy, for example, is little affected by economic booms, recessions, upturns, or downturns. A sick person needs medicine regardless of the economy. Many businesses, though, are subject to the vagaries of the economy. New car dealers and building contractors tend to do well in a good economy, and poorly in a slow economy. In a recession, auto repair and shoe repair businesses thrive—when money is limited, repair is more affordable than replacement. If the economy is in transition, be very careful about making projections based upon past financials for businesses that can be expected to change for better or worse with the economy.

Fair Market Value of Assets

Businesses can deduct most types of its capital expenditures, up to a grand total of $500,000 in 2013.This deduction is subject to a dollar for dollar phase-out, when a business spends over $2,000,000 on total Section 179 expenditures, but many small businesses can manage to accumulate substantial assets without them showing on the balance sheet. That is why you need to adjust to the fair market value of the assets. The value of inventory or work in process may also be understated in a small business. Businesses are able to legitimately choose a method of valuing inventory (LIFO - Last in First out, FIFO – First in First Out, Average Cost for example) that minimizes the value of inventory and reduces taxes.

Customer Concentration

Small businesses are more likely to have significant customer concentration, where a few customers, or possibly even a single customer, account for a significant percentage of the business. As a buyer, insist on some form of a retention guarantee or earn-out if you are buying a business with significant customer concentration.

What is the Business Worth to You?

The methods for valuing a business we've discussed are a good starting point; they tell you what the business is worth to a financial buyer. However, you are a strategic, not a financial buyer. The business has more value to you because of the synergies that you hope to achieve. A money-losing business may be worth nothing to a financial buyer, but if by buying the business and combining its operations with your own company's you can reduce overhead, reduce materials costs, and achieve other efficiencies, the business may quickly become profitable.

To figure out what the business is really worth as a strategic buyer, you need to estimate how the business will likely perform if it were to be combined with your company. We cover how to project future performance and to account for the time value of money in the Discounted Cash Flow section of Chapter VII (Valuation). Be careful not to be too optimistic. For example, we once watched a business forms company buy a software company that served the trade association market. Trade associations were heavy users of preprinted forms such as invoices, membership cards, meeting registration confirmations, etc. onto which the software added personalized information. The form printer assumed that if the company's software already contained templates that allowed the software to easily print onto its standard pre-printed forms, they would be able to gain an audience with the trade associations and displace the existing forms vendor. The additional profits from anticipated increased forms sales were used to justify paying a higher price for the software company than its earnings would have supported. Unfortunately, after the acquisition, they learned that displacing the incumbent forms vendor was harder than they anticipated. The associations often had a lot of their existing forms that they wanted to use up and doing so required changing the software to accommodate their existing forms. The software company would make that change because the alternative was often giving up the sale of the software. Once the change was made, the new form vendor had no advantage over the incumbent. A few years later, the software company was sold back to its former owners.

Another important point when figuring out the value a business has to you is to ensure that you consider all of the costs of merging the two businesses. These costs may include training, moving expenses, time to communicate with customers, and legal costs.

There are many areas in which combining businesses may result in significant cost savings. For example, when purchasing supplies, you may be able to qualify for quantity discounts or otherwise get better terms with higher volumes. You may be able to reduce the total overhead expenses by combining functions such as IT, bookkeeping, and even marketing.

Another way to look at what the business is worth to you is to determine how much it would cost you to achieve the same growth using organic methods. If, for example, you can add $5,000,000 in sales by acquiring a competitor, how much would it cost to achieve that by adding salespeople, expanding your plant, etc.?

Why It's a Mistake to Buy a Business Based On Projections

It is even riskier to buy based on projected performance. In addition to the risk that you overstate the synergies, you must take care not to give away the value of your future work. Let's say that you own a juice company and want to go into the soda business. I may own a cola company, with a great recipe that tastes better than Coke or Pepsi, but if my company is only slightly profitable the recipe is worth little. Should you acquire my cola company and build it into the billion-dollar empire that it can no doubt become, it will largely be because of the hard work, risks, and capital that you invested. You can base your price for my business on how much it would cost to come up with a comparable company or a similar cola recipe (see buy vs. build/ leapfrogging startup in the valuation section), but basing it on the value of your projected success is not fair, because if you do so, I become a partner in your success without needing to do any of the work or take any of the risk. In the event that a seller wants to share in your success, you might consider offering to pay less than the business is worth based on past performance and adding some sort of earn-out so that the seller shares in the risk as well as the reward.

What to Offer Now that You Have Valued the Business

Once you have calculated the value of the business to a financial buyer and to your company, you need to decide what to offer the existing owner. The financial value approximates what a buyer is likely to pay on the open market. The strategic value is the upper limit of what the business is worth to you.

You need to decide how eager the seller is to close a deal, how much of the deal will be cash at close, and how much of the risk you want the seller to retain. For a typical seller on an offer that is mostly paid for with cash at closing, as a rule of thumb, start with the value for a financial buyer and add 5 to 20% of the difference between that value and the higher strategic value. In almost no case should you add more than one times EBITDA to the price that you are paying for a business.

If the cost structure of the acquired business is largely irrelevant to you—for example, if you have a web-hosting company and will move the acquired accounts onto your existing servers, calculate the value based on the value of the customer base. Make sure that you include the costs of moving the customers into your system if you use this methodology. Also, carefully consider the potential effects of the possibility of lower than anticipated rates of customer retention on your valuation.

Marketplace Opportunities

Despite some well-known problems and pitfalls, there is a relatively efficient market for buying ownership shares in public companies. If I want to buy a little piece of Apple Computer or Wal-Mart, or any of thousands of publicly traded companies, I can easily do so. While there is occasional controversy about some buyers getting price advantages over others, the range of variance in share prices at any point in time is quite small. There is also excellent liquidity for selling stock in publicly traded companies. If I have a change of heart as soon as a few minutes after my purchase of Apple or Wal-Mart or another publicly traded company, I can sell it very easily and quickly, most likely with just a very small gain or loss.

Part of the reason that U.S. stock markets work as well as they do is protections designed and enforced by the Securities and Exchange Commission (SEC). Some of those protections involve assuring that no buyers or sellers of a company's stock have access to information that could have a material impact on a stock's value, which others do not have. Those that do have significant information that could impact a company's prospects or stock value are strictly prohibited from trading based on that information, with severe penalties if they are caught doing so.

When it comes to privately held companies, there is no such efficient market. There is no equivalent to the SEC that makes rules to protect either buyer or seller. There is a great deal of liquidity in the stock market. However, there is no such liquidity when you are selling a closely held company. If you buy part or all of a private company and decide you don't want to own it anymore, there is no ready market to go to sell it. You have to search for a buyer, negotiate a price, and hopefully consummate a deal.

There are also not equivalent rules regarding information asymmetry. There are certain disclosure rules, but they only protect against the most egregious offenses. For the most part, a seller is essentially free to trade on the equivalent of inside information regarding his company and industry. The buyer is responsible for doing his own due diligence (see Chapter XII) to determine that the information being represented is true and accurate (and that no essential information is being undisclosed), but there is no SEC type governmental authority that is there to help assure that no information is being suppressed and no misrepresentations are being made.

As a practical matter, a seller knows his business better than the buyer does. A prudent buyer should do his homework and due diligence and still assume that he does not know nearly as much as the seller knows about the company being acquired.

There can also be what we call information asymmetry.

In nearly all instances, a person or institution buying public company stock is doing so for purpose of earning a profit on that purchase. That hoped-for profit may come from dividends or gains in the price that stock fetches when it is resold.

In the case of companies buying companies, the goal is still profit. However, it may not be quite as simple as passively hoping the acquired company generates profits that can be taken in the form of dividends and a future gain in the value of the acquired company. There can be, and likely are, other tactical reasons for the acquisition that are designed to lead to the long-term goal of profitability. These strategic advantages, such as synergies, economies of scale, even the elimination of a competitor(s), are discussed throughout this book.

The point here is that there isn't a generally accepted narrow range of value for a small, privately held company that prospective buyers will agree upon. The value of a company to a buyer can and does vary a great deal depending on each buyer's needs and utilization plans. A financial buyer of a hobby company selling knitting supplies, for example, may look at the earnings of that company, apply a multiplier of 3X or 4X, and set the value range based on that calculation. However, a company that sells similar hobby supplies, quilting supplies, for example, may approach the valuation quite differently. That buyer might reason that he can sell quilting supplies to the target company's knitting customers and knitting supplies to its existing quilting customer base. He can almost immediately increase sales of both knitting supplies and quilting supplies, and gain additional economies of scale (order processing, storage, purchasing, etc.). Therefore, the knitting supply company is very likely to have a much higher value to the quilting company than to the financial buyer, who is approaching it much more like an investor in a public company's stock.

Now, if that knitting supply company is offered for sale for say 3.75 times its annual earnings that may be a steep price for most buyers. But for the fictional quilting company, purchasing it at 4 times or 5 times earnings or more may be a great investment based on the advantages that should accrue to that buyer.

My favorite example of this 2+2= 5 phenomenon is that of payroll service companies. This industry is dominated by large public companies like ADP and Paychex, but there are also a lot of much smaller players. The larger companies have aggressive programs to acquire these smaller companies. In making acquisitions, they really don't care about the standard measures of valuation like earnings. They have developed analytical methods that consider a target company's gross sales, rates, geography, and other factors, and will make an offer based upon the value to the buying company as calculated by their internally developed methodologies. It is not uncommon for a large payroll company to acquire an unprofitable payroll service for 2 times or more of its annual gross fee revenue. In fact, people in the payroll industry know this and will sometimes start companies, gain a few (or a few hundred) clients with the express purpose of selling their company, which really means selling those clients, to a large payroll company buyer.

The payroll example applies to the payroll industry in general. The rationale is essentially that of economies of scale. The incremental cost of servicing an additional client is far less than the incremental income that each additional client produces, as long as the purchasing company has excess capacity. This same rationale applies to a lot of industries: any industry in which an additional client or customer produces a great deal more income than incremental expense.

There are some advantages that are unique to relatively small industries and even to a particular company. For example:

Some years ago, we arranged the purchase of a small company that provided a service to the defense aircraft manufacturing industry. There are only a few prime contractors that manufacture aircrafts for the US Department of Defense. To sell to companies like Boeing, United Technologies, or Lockheed Martin, a vendor needs to be on the contractor's approved vendor list. Our client was not on the list of two of the companies to which they wanted to sell. The client wanted to acquire a company that, among other requirements, was on the approved list of at least one of the companies. Our buyer wanted to acquire a company to provide it a quick entrée to a large potential customer's purchasing department. The company we found for them was on the list of both companies, providing our client with a unique acquisition investment opportunity: a company that had particular value to them, but not to too many others.

Here's an example of a unique advantage that applies to a specific company: Our client company operated a metals distribution company, with some value-added product offerings. As part of its business, the company owned a large and underutilized warehouse. The company was buying many of the metals it distributed from a Canadian company that sold products significantly cheaper than its U.S. competitors. However, this Canadian company's delivery policy was that it would deliver to U.S. customers that were located no more than 75 miles from its plant. Our client was 73 miles from that plant.

They reasoned that if they could find a similar company to acquire that was no more than about two hours south of their warehouse, they could extend their distribution and supply their acquired customers with the Canadian steel, increasing margins considerably. As an added benefit, they could fill their underutilized warehouse and, in essence, store metal for free, or at least for no more cost than they were already paying for the storage facility. We found them just such a company, which they acquired. Three years later, the acquired company's volume has more than doubled and margins have skyrocketed.

If you can find a company that has more value to you than to most other buyers, you may well have an opportunity for a great investment. For example, a target company that can enable you to do one or more of the following may be a great synergistic investment for your company:

- Eliminate a competitor

- Offer access to new markets

- Utilize excess capacity (such as production capacity, storage space, or employee time)

- Gain employees with needed skills or talents

- Gain product or services to sell to existing customers

- Take advantage of several possible economy of scale opportunities

Even better: If you can find a target company that has unique value to your company, such as our client company that was able to redistribute Canadian metals, you have found an excellent investment opportunity.

VIII. Deal Structure

Stock vs. Asset Sale

Assuming that the business being acquired is a corporation, there is a choice in how the deal is structured. The buyer can either acquire the stock or the assets of the firm. There is a clear advantage to the buyer in acquiring the assets of the firm instead of the stock—most liabilities do not follow the assets, and most small business acquisitions are structured as asset sales. In general, acquiring liabilities is not a problem; you just adjust the price to reflect the liabilities that you assume. However, by structuring the transaction as an asset sale, you reduce the chances that you will be responsible for undisclosed or contingent liabilities. Be careful, because existing tax and tort liabilities can follow the assets. If real estate is acquired as part of the transaction, environmental liabilities can also be an issue.

Selling the assets of a corporation generally only requires a majority vote of the shareholders, so even if a minority shareholder objects to the sale and refuses to sell his shares, an asset sale can allow the business to be sold. An asset sale also allows for the sale of only part of the company, although in most cases all of the assets of the corporation are purchased, including the company name, customer lists, etc.

One advantage to a stock sale is that it is easier and less expensive than an asset sale. In an asset sale, the property must be re-titled in the name of the new business and the business name must be transferred. Some contracts and licenses, including leases and customer contracts, may not be transferable to another entity or may require written consent from the other parties to the contracts. In a stock sale, the owners of the company change, but the company itself does not change, so there is no contract transfer issue unless the contract has a clause triggered by a "change of control."

A purchase by corporate stock is often the vehicle of choice if there is to be a partial buyout. If you wanted, for example, to buy 25%, 50%, 60%, or any other proportion of a corporation, you would merely buy that percentage of stock in the corporation. Compared to the alternatives, a stock sale makes partial ownership transition relatively simple.

An asset sale also allows the new owners the flexibility to change accounting methods, including how inventory is valued, cash vs. accrual accounting methods, and depreciation methods. In a stock sale retain their basis and the depreciation schedule is uninterrupted. However, a Section 338(h)(10) Election can be used in a stock saleto treat the sale as an asset sale from the perspective of the corporation and the buyer, even though a stock sale occurred. This allows assets to be stepped up by the purchaser to the price paid for the company plus liabilities assumed plus acquisition costs.

One big advantage from the seller's perspective of structuring the deal as a stock sale is that in a stock sale, the seller clearly leaves behind almost all contingent liabilities, including the threat of future lawsuits. Purchasers are not eager to assume liabilities, so most small business acquisitions are structured as assets sales. With strong representations and warrantees, however, stock sales do happen, especially in businesses where hidden liabilities are unlikely.

Another advantage of a stock sale to the seller is that the profits from the sale are generally taxed at the capital gains rate. Furthermore, if the corporation is structured as a C corporation, an asset sale often results in income that the corporation must pay corporate income tax on and then when the proceeds of the sale are paid out the stockholders are taxed again at their individual tax rates.

Nevertheless, you should make sure that all of the purchased company's creditors are paid. Even if you are not legally liable, you do not want to have conflicts with suppliers, wholesalers, service providers, or others. You can require that money be escrowed to pay creditors.

Tax Consequences

When buying a company, careful consideration needs to be given to the tax consequences of the transactions. From a seller's perspective, there can be a significant impact on how much of the purchase price he can actually keep, based on whether he must pay ordinary income tax or capital gains taxes on the proceeds of the sale. As a buyer, you want to be able to either immediately expense, or quickly depreciate or amortize as much of the purchase price as possible. In our experience, both as intermediaries and principals, the best strategy is one in which both parties cooperate in legally minimizing the total tax burden and negotiate over how to divide the benefits of the taxes that were saved.

S Corporations

In a stock sale, an S Corporation does not pay taxes at the corporate level. The stockholders pay capital gains taxes on the transaction, not ordinary income taxes. Since individual capital gains rates are lower than ordinary income rates, it is clearly in the seller's interest to structure the deal as a stock sale.

In an asset sale however, the tax treatment is less certain. The proceeds from an asset sale must be allocated: an amount for tangible assets, an amount for consulting and non-compete agreements, an amount for goodwill, etc. for tax purposes. The allocation must be reported on IRS form 8594. Both parties must file the form with the IRS. The purchase price is allocated to the assets acquired. The IRS requires that you allocated the purchase price based on the fair market value of the assets being transferred. The buyer will want to allocate the purchase price to items that can be quickly depreciated after the sale. The amount allocated to these items forms the buyer's basis in the items and the buyer can get a fresh start depreciating the assets. However, if more than the depreciated value of items on the seller's balance sheet is allocated to those items, the seller will pay ordinary income tax on the depreciation recapture.

Generally the purchase price is for more than the fair market value of the tangible assets. Once the value of the tangible assets has been determined, the remainder is allocated to intangible assets. When allocating the purchase price it is important to keep in mind that although intangibles, goodwill, and non-compete agreements can all be amortized over 15 years by the buyer, the seller pays only capital gains rate on goodwill, but must pay ordinary income taxes on the non-compete agreement.

Intellectual Property that have a legal life, such as patents, trademarks, or copyrights, are treated as a capital gain for the seller. The buyer can then amortize the intellectual property over the remaining life of the assets. In some cases, a strategy of allocating purchase price to intellectual property may allow the seller to receive a capital gain **and** the buyer to rapidly expense the purchase price.

Consulting or employment agreements are far more favorable to the buyer. They are deductible as an ordinary expense when paid. However, the seller will pay ordinary income tax rates on the income and be subject to FICA.

Limited Liability Corporations (LLCs) can elect to be taxed as either an S Corporation or a C Corporation. They usually have used from 2553 to elect to be treated like S Corporations for tax purposes. Smaller LLCs file as partnerships and may even file a schedule C on an individual return (if there is just a single owner). You need to determine the tax structure of the acquisition target to be certain how the transaction will be taxed, but it is reasonable to initially assume that the transaction will be taxed as if you were acquiring an S corporation.

C Corporations

Buying a C corporation via an asset sale is problematic. The C Corporation pays tax on the goodwill at regular corporate rates, and then the proceeds are taxed again when they are distributed to shareholders. Total taxes can approach 50% of the proceeds. Converting the company from a C corporation to an S Corporation before the sale won't matter; there is a ten-year waiting period during which an asset sale is treated as if the company were still a C Corp.

If a C Corporation must be acquired as an asset sale, there are a few strategies that can reduce the tax rate. Allocating part of the purchase price to covenants not to compete, employment agreements, and personal goodwill can reduce the amount subject to this double taxation.

It is important to note that an asset sale typically includes both tangible and intangible assets of the selling entity. Intangible assets such as customer lists, business name, trademarks, and patents can be, and usually are, part of an asset sale.

Crafting an Offer

It is convenient to liken the process of buying a business to that of buying a house or an investment real estate property. While the analogy is easy to understand, it is also inaccurate in many ways.

There are myriad factors to consider in the mechanics of acquiring a company. There is, of course, the deal structure to consider: That is, what are you buying? Is it a stock sale in which you're buying the stock of a corporation? If so, are you buying 100% of the stock or some lesser percent? Or are you buying the assets? In either case, exactly which assets are included? See Chapters VIII and XI for a discussion of a stock vs. an asset sale.

Then there is the price. How will that price be paid? Will it be all cash at closing, or will some be paid over time? Will some of the price be in the form of owner financing, and if so, on what terms? How much of the payment will be contingent on the future performance of the business? Will the existing owners continue as employees after the closing, and if so, on what terms?

Of course, there will be a period of verification (due diligence), so the buyer can be sure that he is buying what the seller represents that he is selling.

There are several other important details to consider in the somewhat complex process of buying a company. Having just said that, it may sound like a contradiction to say we like to keep the initial offer stage as simple as possible. We advise that buyers submit a non-binding proposal or "term sheet" designed more to establish whether a deal is likely. Such a proposal should outline the buyer's thinking in somewhat broad strokes, recognizing that there are many details that need to be worked out, but establishing the parameters of the negotiations. The seller's response to your non-binding proposal will at least establish whether he is serious about making a deal within the range that you consider reasonable.

Submitting this broad proposal, rather than specifying all issues, at this early stage can potentially save a lot of time and money. For example, suppose you determine that a particular target is worth $1,000,000 to your company and you need the owner to remain on as manager of the company he now owns for at least a year under your ownership. You submit a proposal at say $900,000 (figuring you're open to going up on price to $1,000,000) with a stipulation that owner stays on for at least a year full time. Based on your attorney's advice, you specify an asset sale. The buyer, on the other hand, insists on a minimum of $1,600,000 and a stock sale (based on his accountant's advice), and a commitment to remain six months maximum. Well, you've spent a few hours putting together a proposal and learned that a deal is not going to happen. That's unfortunate, but it's a lot better than having spent many more hours and many dollars on accountant and lawyer fees working out all the details for a deal that isn't getting beyond the starting gate.

If, on the other hand, the seller responds with $1.1 Million as the selling price, and saying he's open to an asset sale with as long as a few other conditions are met and that he'd be happy to stay for at least a year, then we're in the ballpark, and further discussions are merited.

A few tips regarding your initial proposal:

• Make sure it's non-binding. State clearly, "This document is for discussion purposes only and not binding on either party." It would be a good idea to run the document by your lawyer first to make absolutely sure you are not committing to anything you don't wish to commit to. But don't let your lawyer talk you into a full-fledged detailed offer at this point.

• For now, assume that everything you have been told is true. You can prepare your non-binding proposal based on this assumption as long as you make it clear that your proposal is based on the information presented to you and that no deal will go forward until and unless you verify that what has been presented to you is true and accurate to your satisfaction. This verification process is called "due diligence." It will come after you have agreed on the major terms of the deal.

• Keep it simple and stay away from legal language. We've seen more than one deal get into trouble at this early stage simple because the seller didn't understand the buyer's proposal. Your proposal here is for discussions between prospective buyer and prospective seller. There is plenty of time to translate your plain language agreement into legal language and to address the myriad of details later.

When presenting the price we like to present the total potential price and then break it down based on terms. For example:

> **Proposed Purchase Price**. MyCo will agree to buy 100% of the Stock of the Company for total consideration of $20,000,000 which will be paid as follows:
>
> (i) $10,000,000 in cash at closing and;
>
> (ii) $1,000,000 in equity representing 2.0%

ownership in MyCo; and

(iii) A cash escrow of $1,000,000. The escrow will be held for any future claims. If there are no claims the escrow will be released eighteen (18) months following closing.

(iv) $2,000,000 in a note payable over 60 months with a 7% interest rate

(v) $1,000,000 in the form of assuming the mortgage on the property at 123 Main Street

(vi) A dollar for dollar earn-out up to $5,000,000 to the Sellers based upon NewCo generating from $9,000,000 to $14,000,000 of EBITDA in the first year after closing.

Potential terms are discussed in detail below in the LoI Section.

It is our longstanding belief that many, if not most sellers don't really know what they will or won't accept until a proposal is placed in front of them. Remember that selling one's business is often at least as much an emotional undertaking as it is a financial transaction. Unfortunately, it sometimes takes an actual proposal for the seller to realize he is not really a seller at all. Conversely, we have seen situations where a proposal has demonstrated to a prospective seller that selling at a favorable price is a real possibility and he gets more excited and more serious about the prospect of selling and moving on to the next life phase. We see the non-binding proposal as the gateway to discovering whether a deal is a genuine possibility. If such a proposal is positively received, then serious discussions and negotiations can follow.

Letter of Intent

Assuming your non-binding proposal meets with a positive response, presumably after a bit of back and forth, the next step is to prepare a more formal document known as a letter of intent (LoI). While most LoIs provide the buyer with an "out," it is a somewhat more formal document than the proposal discussed above. Therefore, we strongly recommend that you don't submit a LoI until your lawyer has reviewed it. Note that some experienced buyers often start with the LoI instead of the proposal that we recommend.

The LoI is basically a formal version of the proposal with the modifications as agreed to by the parties. While a LoI is a long way from a closing, it is a legal document that commits the parties to certain steps and restrictions, and it defines, or at least outlines the steps that will be taken toward the closing.

We advise that you put the agreed terms in writing in plain English first and let your lawyer revise it as necessary, adding necessary protections for you.

The letter of intent is a detailed outline of the deal. While LoIs vary, most include the following stipulations

- Price
- Payment terms
- Target closing date
- Contingencies (i.e. deal may be dependent on financing such that if buyer can't obtain financing; deal can be cancelled without penalty)
- Stipulation for due diligence (as a contingency)
- Initial deposit (if any)
- Restrictions on the seller against further marketing of the business for a stated period of time
- and probably more, depending on the situation

Price

The price that you pay is obviously very important to the success of the deal. Determining a reasonable price is covered in detail in Chapter VII.

Payment Terms

The terms of a deal can be as important as the price. The right terms may allow you to reduce the total amount that you pay, to finance part of the purchase with earnings from the business that you acquire, and to have the seller retain some of the risk for a period of time.

Seller Provided Notes

Will the owner be taking back paper to finance part of the deal? What interest rate will you pay on the note? What collateral is required to secure the note? From your perspective as a buyer, the business itself would be a good thing to pledge as security. Should it turn out that the business had really severe problems that you somehow missed, you can give it back and lose only the down payment. A seller, on the other hand, will see things differently; he's handing you a money-making business and if you mess it up he doesn't want a money-losing business back, so he may want additional security.

Earn Out Provisions

You may be able to have the current owner accept some of the purchase price in the form of an earn-out provision. In this scenario, you offer a percentage of sales or profits (typically gross profits) for some period of time after the sale.

Claw-backs

These are rare, but can be useful in certain situations. Usually, they are used to deal with situations in which the purchase of a particular business has an extraordinary risk associated with it. Here are a couple of examples:

Example 1: A purchaser is buying a business where 80% of the sales are from three large customers. The seller assures the buyer that the business has solid relationships with these customers and that they are unlikely to leave, but the buyer is wary. Forty percent of the purchase price is placed in an escrow account and paid out to the seller in 24 equal monthly payments. In the event that a major customer fires the company in the first two years, the money that remains in the escrow account is paid out to the buyer.

Example 2: We were selling a construction company that had a large number of unionized employees who participated in a multi-employer pension plan through their union. During due diligence the buyer discovered that the pension plan was underfunded and that if the company were to withdraw from the plan it would face a $4,000,000 withdraw liability. The seller argued that the liability was a contingent liability, which would only become an actual liability if the company terminated the pension plan. He further argued that the underfunding was largely a result of the market crash in 2008 and was likely to disappear as the market recovered. The solution was a seller financed note that allowed the buyer to claw back part of the purchase price if the liability did not shrink during the five years after the sale.

Non-compete Agreements

You do not want to buy a business only to find that the former owner opens a competing establishment that limits the prospects of the business that you just acquired. To make sure that this does not happen, you include a covenant not to compete in the purchase and sale agreement.

A covenant not to compete cannot be so broad as to make it impossible (or nearly impossible) for the former owner to make a living, or a court will hold it to be unenforceable. Generally, courts won't modify the agreement—they'll just throw it out entirely, meaning the seller can now compete as he likes. So, you want to craft it in a way that makes it difficult for the former owner to compete without making the former owner unemployable. How you craft it depends on the nature of the business that you are buying. For example, if you were purchasing a dry cleaning business where most of the customers were local, you might design a non-compete agreement that prevented the owner from working for a retail business within 50 miles of any location of the dry cleaning business that you are buying. By contrast, if you are buying a software company that makes software for colleges and universities worldwide, the covenant might restrict the former owner's employment by any company that derives a substantial portion of its revenues from providing software to educational institutions.

Target Closing Date

Choose a target closing date that allows sufficient time for due diligence, acquiring bank financing, and other needed tasks. Consult your lawyer and accountant about time needed to perform these steps. Generally, closing happens 60 to 100 days after the LoI is signed.

Contingencies

The LoI can be made contingent on the ability to raise funds for the acquisition, results of Phase I or Phase II environmental assessments, assuring that the business contracts are transferable, and any other event that needs to occur for the buyer to be comfortable closing the transaction. Acceptable performance in due diligence is required and usually "acceptable" is defined as at the sole discretion of the buyer, allowing the buyer to back out easily (see below).

Stipulation for Due Diligence

Technically, due diligence is a contingency, but one that deserves its own category. Virtually all LoIs grant the buyer the right to verify that all that was represented to him regarding the selling company is accurate and complete. The items that are examined during due diligence includes financial information (going back several years) and much more. It is the buyer's right, indeed his responsibility, to examine all aspects of the business he is about to acquire. The severity of this stipulation varies. In some instances it will state that the buyer may cancel the deal, for example, if he finds material inaccuracies in due diligence. In other cases, the buyer may cancel the deal based on anything he learns in due diligence that doesn't meet his approval. Be careful that the due diligence language is broad enough to allow you to cancel or renegotiate the deal without penalty if you find any surprises that will impact on the company's value or suitability for your intended purpose for making the acquisition.

Initial Deposit (if any)

Often, a small amount of money (maybe 5% of the purchase price) is deposited in escrow with either the buyer's or the seller's lawyer.

The deposit is usually fully refundable if the buyer is unhappy with anything that he discovers during the due diligence period. The money serves as an indicator that the buyer is serious and committed to closing the transaction.

Restrictions on the Seller against Further Marketing of the Business for a Stated Period of Time

The LoI usually requires that the seller take the company off the market as soon as it is signed. This means that the seller must cease negotiations with other potential buyers. The seller can resume marketing the business if either the buyer indicates that he wants to back out of the transaction because one of the contingencies is not satisfied or if the closing does not occur by the stated date.

The stipulations discussed above are the most common ones that are contained in almost every LoI for a business acquisition. Depending on the situation, there can be many other LoI stipulations and requirements. A LoI is a legal document that binds the buyer and the seller in several ways. That is why we recommend that you don't sign a LoI without obtaining the advice of an attorney experienced in business acquisitions.

Payment in Stock

You may be able to interest the seller in taking some, or all, of the purchase price in the form of stock in the combined entity or stock in the acquired company (if it will continue to be operated as a separate legal entity). If you want to convince the seller to accept equity, the first question is how much equity do you want the seller to retain? If either party holds a minority interest, it will want assurances that its interests will still be respected. A majority shareholder can pay himself (or his family members) an inflated salary, make purchases from or sales to other companies that he owns at prices that are inflated, or engage in any number of other methods to deprive the minority shareholder of fair value. To ensure that this does not happen the offer will often contain a big stick that the minority shareholder can use—allowing the minority shareholder to force a sale of the entire company, for example. Other decisions may require a super-majority vote of shareholders.

The scenario in which the seller retains equity works best if the seller will continue to play a substantial role in the ongoing operation of the business and is expected to have a material impact on its success.

Deal Details

Real Estate

Often, a business includes significant real estate holdings. While it might be advantageous to acquire the real estate as part of the transaction, there are a number of scenarios in which it might make more sense to allow the seller to retain the real estate and sign a lease at closing, leasing the real estate back from the seller. After all, you want to invest in the business, not speculate on property values. You need to consider how integral the real estate is to the operation of the business, how important the location is, and what it would cost to move the business.

If you decide to acquire real estate, it is vital that you understand any environmental and zoning issues, and have the real estate and buildings independently inspected and appraised. Alternatively, if you allow the seller to retain the real estate, you need to negotiate a lease that is signed as part of the closing process.

Transferring Current Assets and Liabilities

There will always be current assets and liabilities when you close a deal. Generally, cash and cash equivalents are retained by the seller. However, the accounts receivable and payable can be more complex.

With all but a few cash businesses, whenever you close there will be accounts receivable. The seller will usually want to include the receivables as part of the sale since it will be easier for you to collect them, both in terms of having staff and because customers will not want to harm the ongoing relationship with you; the seller gets the cash immediately at close, and the buyer then assumes the credit risk. However, paying for the account receivables at closing increases the cost of the acquisition and exposes you to credit risk. On the other hand, having the seller retain A/R draws customers' attention to the ownership change and can result in customer confusion about which invoice is due to which party, and the seller may have issues cashing checks since the business name is usually included in the sale.

A reasonable compromise on the treatment of Accounts Receivable is to have the seller retain the A/R, but have the buyer agree to collect them on the seller's behalf. The agreement may need to specify how payments that are received will be treated—should a payment be applied to oldest balance vs. applied to a recent invoice whose dollar total is the same as the amount of the payment, for example. The agreement should also specify how often the buyer will remit collected funds to the seller, specifics about what type of services and reporting will be provided, and what charges, if any, the buyer can charge for the collection services.

There will also be accounts payable at closing. Usually, the seller is responsible for A/P up to the day of closing. Bills that span the closing date (utility, phone, etc.) are pro-rated. A small amount of money from the closing price can be left in escrow and used to reimburse the buyer for A/P that the buyer pays, for which the seller is responsible. After some period of time (60 to 90 days) any funds remaining in the escrow account are distributed to the seller.

Customer Retention

If the business has significant customer concentration, where a few customers are responsible for the bulk of the sales, or the primary value of the business is the customer base that is being acquired as in the payroll service example, then the deal may require a customer retention clause. This allows the buyer to mitigate the risk of acquiring the business only to see the customers leave. Customer retention may be guaranteed by escrowed funds or an earn-out provision.

Employment Contracts

As a buyer, you may want to include employment contracts as part of the purchase. Contracts can be used to lock in key employees, including the seller. A generous employment contract may be a way to sweeten an offer without requiring additional cash up front. The employment agreement also allows the seller to feel comfortable that he won't be forced out after closing.

Dealing with Multiple Owners

Many businesses, even small ones, have more than one owner. When trying to deal with multiple owners, it is important to determine whether all of the major owners are truly willing to sell. If a major owner, especially one that is active in the business, does not want to sell, his objection can easily scuttle the deal. If possible, meet with all of the owners relatively early in the process and assess their commitment to doing a transaction. It can be helpful to pose questions such as "Do you want to retain some equity?" to guide you in proposing a deal structure that will be acceptable to the various owners.

We have seen professional buyers insist before entering into negotiations that all owners agree to allow a single shareholder to vote their shares on issues related to the transaction. This approach can work when dealing with a family owned business, where shareholders can rely on one family member to act in their best interest, but is impractical in a situation with many unrelated shareholders.

Purchase and Sale Agreement

After the LoI is signed, both parties have agreed legally and in principle to consummate a deal assuming that all contingencies are met and that due diligence results are satisfactory to the buyer. Invariably, there will be some issues that need to be ironed out after the LoI is signed and before the P&S is signed, but the momentum is toward finalizing the acquisition as defined in the LoI.

Often, the lawyers will be working on the Purchase and Sale agreement while due diligence is being carried out (see below).

IX. Negotiating the Deal

Negotiating to buy a business is not different from other kinds of negotiations. There are books, courses, and programs available on negotiating techniques that can help you if you feel you need help. This section will cover some of the important elements of the process specifically as they relate to acquiring a business.

Think Like the Seller

Before entering into a buy/sell negotiation, try to put yourself in the seller's position. While you may think that the asking price is far from reasonable, consider how the seller feels. He may intellectually understand that you are not concerned about the work of the past, but rather about the future potential. However, this business represents years of labor and risk. Emotionally, selling the business represents at least the closing of a chapter of his life. The deal that is finally consummated determines the sweetness or bitterness of the close of that chapter. The more you can appreciate where the seller is coming from, the better you will be able to handle the negotiating process.

Be Polite and Respectful from the Start

Business owners are very sensitive about their businesses. The worst thing you can do is to give the seller the message that you think he mismanaged the business and that you can easily improve the operation. It is far more productive to compliment the seller where you can, and keep your negative observations to yourself. Good feelings about a prospective buyer can be incredibly important to a deal's success. On the other hand, buyer insensitivity to an owner can destroy a deal before it has had a chance to develop.

Do not Insult the Seller with a Low Ball Offer

Some amateur negotiators reason that the lower the original offer, the better. After all, the reasoning continues, "I can always increase the offer." However, the sale of a business is too emotional for the seller for that strategy to work well. If your offer is too far from an acceptable range, he or she may walk away and refuse to even talk about it anymore. We have seen more than one seller get so insulted by a low offer that they sold their businesses to someone else for less than the insulting prospective buyers eventually offered. It is a good idea to discuss, or at least hint at, the price range you will offer before actually making an offer. By doing so, the seller will at least have a general understanding of what to expect. As a rule of thumb, offer no more than fifteen percent lower than you are prepared to pay. Often, it is a better strategy to negotiate on terms rather than on price where possible (see Impasse Busting below).

Even if the seller is not displaying much emotion, but is acting entirely rational, the seller may decide, based on your initial lowball offer, that the odds that you will close a deal are low. Just as you may walk away from a seller that asks far too much for his company, deciding that it is likely that there are better uses for your time than trying to bridge a huge gap, a seller may decide that running his business or looking for other potential buyers is a better use of his time than trying to close a deal with someone who initially far undervalued his business.

Every Seller has other Deals Pending

It is a common strategy for sellers to tell buyers that they have other deals that they are considering. They, of course, do this to pressure you, to extract concessions, and to get you to move faster. Sometimes it's true, sometimes it's not true, and most times it's somewhere in between. That is, a seller may be quick to point out how he received three offers, but not so quick to point out that none of them was even in the ballpark of acceptability. Our advice in general is to brush off talk of other prospects. You don't know how true it may be, and even if you do there is very little that you can do to control what happens with other deals. However, needless delay will only enhance the possibility that another deal will become a threat to you.

Keep Emotions out of Negotiations

It is advisable to use an intermediary in the negotiating process to ensure that emotions don't get in the way of striking the best deal possible. An intermediary such as a business broker (not the same one who is already part of the deal as the seller's agent) or another knowledgeable advisor will be less emotionally invested in the process and better able to negotiate effectively.

Look for Win-Win Negotiation

The old school of thought of negotiating was that every negotiation had a winner and loser, defined by who got the best deal. The modern school of thought is that both sides can come up winners; there does not have to be a loser. Both the buyer and seller can get what they want without defeating the other party. You may be prepared to pay $20,000,000 for a business. That may be a great price if, for example, it would cost far more than that to start your own company and develop it to the point of profitability that the seller has already attained. It may also be a great deal for the seller if he started it for $200,000, he's ready to retire, and he has calculated that as long as he gets over $10,000,000 for the business, his retirement and legacy are financially secure.

Striving for a win-win negotiation lessens the chance of destructive friction and of a full breakdown of negotiations. Of course you won't agree on every point. But you can think in terms of looking for ways to make all parties involved feel that they are getting most of what they want.

Impasse Busting—Negotiate Terms

Sometimes sellers will decide on a price and refuse to sell for a dollar less. If you run into this situation, keep in mind that it is human nature to avoid going back on one's resolution. Instead of negotiating on price, concentrate on terms. For example, "I'll consider paying your price, but let's talk about payment terms. Can you consider financing 35% of the deal at 1 point below prime?" A scenario like this, if accepted, means that the seller does not have to back down, and the buyer gets the net effect of a lower price anyway. You can also try to use non-cash sweeteners in lieu of a higher price. Some non-cash sweeteners include:

- Providing free or cheap use of office space for the seller after the sale.
- Allocation of purchase price in a manner that decreases the seller's tax liabilities.
- Secretarial and related assistance on an occasional basis.
- Discounts on the company's products or services for the seller's family.

- Allowing the seller to keep assets that you don't need.
- Part time employment for the seller's children.
- Increasing the security on seller financing.

Don't Get Bogged Down on Small Points

We have, on more than one occasion, been involved in negotiations that would look silly to an outsider. There have been situations where buyer and seller have come to terms on an eight-figure sell price, but argue about who needs to pay for a few thousand dollars' worth of accrued vacation time. Perhaps arguing the small points relieves the tensions of the negotiation. That's fine. However, be careful not to let a very small point wreck the whole deal or distract attention from substantive issues. During negotiating sessions, we have often suggested dropping a point and coming back to it later if we feel it is relatively insignificant and is bogging down discussions. When we do this, the buyer and seller often forget all about the point that was causing such bitter debate until we bring it up again, often with a proposed simple and fair solution.

Don't Renegotiate Settled Points

Once you have agreed on the outlines of a deal, do not keep re-opening the negotiations to see if you can do better. There is a temptation to say, "I'll bet the seller won't throw away the deal over a small change," and for a while that will be true with most sellers. We have had a seller walk away in disgust from negotiations with a buyer after he repeatedly re-opened deals that he'd agreed to. That seller decided to run his business remotely, rather than sell it.

The exceptions to the rule are if the seller asks for a concession, springs a major surprise on you, or the condition of the business materially changes. In those situations it is entirely reasonable to ask for an adjustment.

Blame Lawyers, Brokers, Brothers, Advisors, Accountants

A common but effective ploy used in negotiating the sale of a business is to blame another person as the bad guy. It's used like this: "I'd agree to pay your price, but my accountant just won't let me do it." Or, "I trust your inventory count, but the bank insists that we do a physical count on closing day." You can always be the good guy while one of your advisors or associates is making all the tough demands. This strategy is especially useful if you will continue to work with the former owner and you need his or her continued cooperation. The advisor can be the whipping boy, while the principals to the deal preserve their friendly relationship.

Chapter Summary

A buy/sell transaction often involves an emotionally charged negotiation. While emotions can be expected to run high, it is best to keep discussions as business-like as possible. Intermediaries may help achieve this. Sometimes impasses can be broken by negotiating terms rather than price, and by offering non-cash sweeteners. Finally, your goal should be a win-win, not a win-lose negotiation.

X. How to Kill a Deal

Lots of deals that are discussed never happen. In many cases, it's for the best that they don't. But in some cases, deals that should happen do not, and often because of mistakes made by the buyer.

Here are some of the things we have seen (and continue to see) that can kill a deal:

Early Deal Killers

Not Respecting the Seller

Probably the best way to kill a deal early on is to show disrespect to the seller. While few buyers would do so intentionally, some do so unintentionally by not understanding entrepreneurial sensitivities. When we see this early deal killer, it usually takes the form of a buyer communicating the attitude of "I know more about business than you do and therefore I can run your business better than you can." No, we've never heard anyone actually say it in quite those words, but we've seen the attitude come across quite clearly.

For example, we've seen buyers take a 10-minute walk through a company with the owner, and then talk for another ten minutes, and say something like, "You need to do radio advertising to increase sales." The owner, who has been running the business for, say, 20 years, probably has a pretty good sense of what works and what doesn't. However, even if he doesn't, and even if radio advertising would greatly increase his business, he certainly doesn't want someone with 10 minutes experience with his business telling him he knows how to run his business better than he's running it.

Another scenario we've witnessed all too often is a buyer trying to dazzle a seller by demonstrating his mastery of sophisticated financial concepts. Many small business owners, including very successful ones, are by nature operations people and not financial experts. They rightly leave financial management issues to their CPAs or to others with financial expertise. Someone coming in and delivering a lecture about how the business should use more leverage or factor their AR, whether the advice is good or bad, is another way to insult a seller and put a deal in early jeopardy.

We are currently in the process of selling a $20MM manufacturing company with an operating profit of well over $2MM. The owner, whom we'll call Keith, knows very well how to operate his company, but he is not an expert in financial management. We had a conference call with a prospective private equity buyer. At the beginning of the conference call, we asked the buyer to give Keith a very brief overview of his company and his possible interest in Keith's company. He went on for a good ten minutes talking about leveraged financing, turns of EBITDA, times interest earned, and various ratios. He finally asked Keith if he had any questions. Keith responded, "Well, I don't understand a word you just said, but that's okay, do you have any questions about my business?" Needless to say, that deal went nowhere with that buyer.

Complexity

Some deals are complex right from the beginning because they need to be. Others become progressively more complex as the deal moves through the process. While no buy-sell deal is simple, many don't need to be extremely complex. An axiom around our office is that the more complex a deal is at the beginning, the less likely that it will close. Small business owners, for whatever reason, just tend to distrust complex deals that they can't readily understand. They tend to want to see a deal spelled out, at least initially, in a page or two. The more likely the initial proposal needs to be deciphered and explained to a seller by his lawyer, the less likely the deal will go forward. The initial proposal should be as simple as is reasonable, even if it means stating that some issues will need to be figured out later in the process.

Later Deal Killers

Owner as Employee

In most acquisitions, the buyer's company and the seller will have to work together for a period of time from a few months to several years. Both buyer and seller are overtly or covertly evaluating the degree to which this working together will work out.

Entrepreneurs often become entrepreneurs because they don't want to answer to a boss. So after five, 10, or 20 years of not having a boss, it's easy to see how they approach having to answer to someone with skepticism and trepidation. In some cases, sellers have an exaggerated view of what having a boss will be like. We often explain to sellers that the purchasing company needs their expertise and very much wants to keep them happy. Yes, after the sale, the old owner may have a boss, but it won't be in the sense that someone will be looking over his shoulder and telling him what to do all day. It will be more like setting goals and meeting periodically to discuss progress toward those goals and business strategy in general.

Nevertheless, sellers who are used to being in full control of their business do sometimes have difficulty with losing, or even sharing that control. In extreme cases, this dynamic can cause a seller to change his mind.

Conversely, many buyers assume that an owner will be unwilling or unable to accept direction because they are used to being the boss. However, most entrepreneurs that have been successful have had to work for customers, who are in effect their bosses. The most successful business people often have a demonstrated ability to work with, accept suggestions from, and compromise with others. Before assuming that the seller will be unable to work as part of a larger organization, look at how he works with employees, customers, suppliers, and advisors, like his accountant and lawyer.

You need to be sure that the seller will be comfortable with your company's culture and that you will be comfortable with him. If there is not mutual respect and *good chemistry*, the deal may not happen, and frankly, that may be better than a deal happening if after the deal the buyer and seller don't get along.

Making Changes and New demands

Letters of intent are agreements in principle that more or less bind the parties to work toward a definitive agreement. Typically, there are refinements, additional details, and changes between the signing of the LoI and signing of the more detailed and definitive purchase and sale agreement. While lawyers fully understand this, sellers often do not. Remember: the sale of a business carries a good deal of emotion for most sellers. They tend to be apprehensive throughout the process and requested changes to the LoI. Making new demands, even seemingly innocuous ones, feed into that apprehension. If you need to make changes, approach the seller with appropriate tact. Intermediaries can be very helpful because they know the process. They know that changes and new details will come up, and they know how to communicate the changes to jittery buyers.

Due Diligence Details

When we are dealing with a seller, we warn him early in the process that the due diligence phase will be laborious, time consuming, and definitely not fun. Buyers and their lawyers and CPAs will be asking for documents some of which are arcane and irreverent as far as the seller is concerned. Despite our warning, sellers are frequently taken aback when they get the due diligence list from the buyer or the buyer's representative. The size of the request alone is daunting. Here, again, an intermediary can be helpful in assisting the seller in gathering the requested information and in explaining why it is important to the seller.

Despite the seller's dislike of the due diligence process, it is obviously essential. However, buyers should understand that entrepreneurs are often not the best record keepers. Keep the due diligence request as lean as is reasonable. If a few documents are missing (and they will be), evaluate whether the missing documents are really important before digging in your heels and insisting the seller find a particular invoice from four years ago for $235. Even IRS auditors exercise a degree of latitude and understanding for a few missing documents.

Talking to Customers or Employees Prematurely (Breaching Confidentiality)

A common point of disagreement between buyer and seller at this stage is that of meeting customers and employees. Buyers, with good reason, want to have a few conversations with key employees and with a few customers. Sellers, with equally good reason, adamantly don't want those conversations to take place, at least not until the deal is nearly finalized. Sellers fear that if customers know the business is for sale they may take their business elsewhere, and employees who are uncomfortable with the uncertainties of how a sale will affect them may start looking for new jobs. To make matters worse, word can get out and rumors can start, which could do real damage to the business.

Usually, these issues are worked out in a way that satisfies both seller and buyer. Until they are, do not violate confidentiality by talking to customers, employees, or anyone else about the pending transaction. Doing so may result in a lawsuit. Even if there is not threat of legal action, breaching confidentiality in this way can absolutely destroy the trust between buyer and seller and easily jeopardize the deal.

Outside Deal Killers

Wives, husbands, fathers, mothers, uncles, aunts, friends and others can and do influence a business owner's decision to sell or not sell. Sometimes that advice is quite reasonable and out of the domain of buyer or intermediary. If, for example, a seller's spouse is concerned about how the sale of the business might affect family dynamics, that is a reasonable concern that should be worked out within the family.

Sellers also too often get advice that is as harmful as it is nonsensical. For example, a friend or relative with no expertise in buying and selling businesses and no grasp of the company's financial picture may tell the seller, "I think your business is worth twice what they're offering," or, "I heard that my friend's sister's boyfriend sold his tiny business to Google for $40,000,000 so yours is worth at least that much." Of course a seller wants to believe he is getting a good deal. But the idea that someone out there might offer him a better deal is very seductive, albeit probably neither logical nor true. All you can really do is appeal to the seller's sense of business logic and explain that he and his professional advisors know better than his well-meaning friends and relatives. That brings us to outside advisors.

Professionals, accountants, and lawyers in particular can squelch a deal. Some are well versed in the esoteric elements in transacting a privately held company, and some are not. Those that are can be very helpful in shepherding a deal along, and even minimize obstacles and expense. If the seller's professional advisors are not experienced with business buying and selling, don't be too surprised if they give questionable advice. For example, his CPA decides that the acquisition price is way too low based on logic that applies to large publicly traded firms. Also, don't be surprised if a seller's attorney tries to, say, decide he needs to protect his client and turn contingency payments such as earn outs into guaranteed payments. Never mind that you and the seller agreed to earn outs as a solution to an issue that was jeopardizing the whole deal. In most situations, these professionals, though they may grandstand a little, understand the logic of the deal and of deal making, and differences can be worked out. We like to engage the seller's accountant early in the process, partly to avoid surprising him at the LoI stage, but partly because he may well be in the best position to answer financial questions that invariably will come up. The seller's CPA will also know his client's tax and overall financial situation and can help structure the deal based on that understanding.

It is worth noting that the sale of a company is probably not good news to its outside professionals. It may well mean the loss of a client. Most accountants and lawyers are fully capable and willing to do the best job they can for their client despite the fact that success may be rewarded by the loss of that client. If you are open to keeping the company's lawyer and or accountant, it couldn't hurt for you to mention that possibility.

XI. Legal Issues

It is essential that you consult an attorney before buying a business and before signing any significant legally binding documents. However, it is generally not necessary to bring your lawyer into the acquisition process until you are ready to make an offer. Your lawyer will have a major role in the process once an offer is made.

Some of the legal issues involved in buying a company are outlined below:

Stock Versus Asset Sale

One way that you can buy a corporation is through the purchase of shares of its stock. In this scenario, you would keep the corporate structure of the acquired company. The stock that the owners of the selling company own would be sold to you for the agreed upon price and terms. The legally created entity of the corporation would continue under the new owner.

Another way to buy a company is on an asset sale basis. In an asset sale, you would buy some or all of the firm's tangible and intangible assets such as equipment, patents, customer lists, business name, and goodwill; shares of stock do not change hands. The existing business, which can be an individual, partnership, or corporation or another type of entity, sells the assets to the buyer. To add a layer of protection against possible liability, lawyers often advise buyers to set up a corporation to buy the assets.

See Chapters VIII and XI for a discussion of buying a company on a stock sale vs. an asset sale basis.

Buying Unincorporated Companies

There is no reason why a person or entity cannot purchase a proprietorship. An unincorporated company must either be purchased on an asset basis, or it must first be incorporated and then sold on a corporate stock basis.

Liens and Encumbrances

A bank or other lender or creditor of your target business may have placed a lien against property owned by the business, by the owner personally, or both. Placing a lien means in essence that the encumbered property can't legally be sold without either paying the indebtedness or otherwise negotiating a release of the encumbrance with the creditor. Banks will often take out a blanket lien on all the property of a corporation to protect their position.

If you are not sure about whether there are encumbrances placed on the company or associated property that you are considering, check with the secretary of state's office in your state, the city or town in which the owner lives, and the city or town where the target business is located. Your attorney can arrange to have a lien search performed and a report delivered to you.

While the cleanest way to get a lien removed is to pay the indebtedness, it may be possible to make other arrangements. For example, a lender might let you assume the lien and the responsibility for the debt upon closing. It is not unusual for a closing to take place with the seller immediately taking the proceeds from the sale and paying off indebtedness, thereby releasing encumbrances. Your lawyer and the seller's lawyer must decide how to remove any existing liens to assure that the business is acquired free and clear of encumbrances, or to decide on a strategy for transferring ownership with the new owner assuming the debt and the liens.

Letter of Intent

A letter of intent (LoI) states that an individual or entity intends to take a certain action (purchasing a company in whole or part) under a certain set of circumstances. We think of it as an agreement to work toward a more definitive agreement. Letters of Intent are discussed in detail in Chapter VIII.

Due Diligence

A letter of intent will almost certainly include a contingency regarding verification. You (or your advisors) will have the right to examine the books, legal agreements, market data, and other information that is relevant to the company you intend to acquire. This examination process is called the due diligence process. As a buyer, you have the responsibility to exercise due diligence or appropriate care and caution, in investigating the seller's property, records, financial data, market data, etc.

The due diligence process must be carried out carefully. While it is the seller's responsibility to provide the information, it is the buyer's responsibility to examine and evaluate the information presented. If the seller provides the information without withholding damaging facts, and you do not properly evaluate the information, it will be very difficult for you to later initiate a claim of misrepresentation after the business changes hands.

No seller, no matter how well-meaning, can provide you with every detail about his business, and even well-intentioned sellers may put an optimistic spin on the facts. For example, we recently sold a manufacturing company with very volatile earnings. The management team was not very sophisticated and could not give a good explanation of the earnings volatility. I determined that the swings in earnings were caused by large engineering contracts from customers that wanted new customized products created. The buyer, however, never asked about the pipeline of future engineering contracts, which meant that the deal closed with the buyer having a far poorer forecast of future earnings than could have been the case.

Purchase and Sale Agreement

The purchase and sale agreement (P&S) is the formal contract that details the terms of the sale. In the case of an asset purchase, it may be referred to as an Asset Purchase Agreement (APA). In either case, it is often drafted and reviewed by the buyer's and seller's attorneys during due diligence, and finalized and executed by the parties once due diligence is complete.

The purchase and sale agreement (or asset purchase agreement) will generally cover the following points:

(1) What is being sold?

(2) When is the buyer taking over the business? (closing date)

(3) The purchase price and (i) how and (ii) when it is to be paid.

(4) What security is the buyer is providing to the seller for any deferred payments that may be involved?

(5) Operation of the business during the interim between the signing a purchase and sale agreement and the closing.

(6) Non-compete agreement.

(7) Warranties by the seller to the buyer, as well as warranties by the buyer to the seller.

(8) Other adjustments.

(9) Contingencies.

Each of these points is addressed below.

Note that many business acquisitions involve a number of ancillary documents along with the Purchase & Sale agreement or Asset Purchase Agreement. For example, lease agreements, non-compete agreements, owner financing agreements, and so on, though integral to the deal, are often drafted as separate agreements that are executed along with the main purchase agreement.

What is Being Bought?

To say you are buying a business is fine for casual conversation. From a legal perspective, however, it is not enough. Lawyers for both sides will insist that the tangible and intangible specifics of the transaction be spelled out in detail. Are you buying a corporation, or are you buying assets (see discussion in Chapters VIII and XI, stock versus assets sale)? If it's a stock sale, the number of shares being sold and the price per share is delineated, along with several other details. If you are buying assets, which assets are you buying? What about the liabilities? Will you take them over, or will the seller be responsible for them?

Also, the sale must be carefully allocated for tax purposes, as discussed in Chapter VIII.

Closing Date

In most situations (and to over simplify a bit), the formal business-buying process is a two-part process. In one part, the purchase and sale agreement that was carefully negotiated while due diligence was occurring is signed and funds are transferred; in the other, usually hours after the documents are signed and funds are transferred, the business is taken. One of the reasons for this two-stage arrangement is the need to take inventory. In a business that has a material amount of inventory, the inventory may change from day to day, even while the sale is being executed. Most often you will agree to a price on the assumption that the inventory is at a certain level. The agreement should state the assumed level and how the price will be adjusted if the level is different based on an actual count on closing day. In most cases, the buyer and seller agree to a price for the business and a date on which the business will change hands. A lot of business closings take place on Monday so inventory can be taken over the preceding weekend.

Price - Payment Terms, Security

As discussed in a number of areas in this book, price and terms for a business transaction can be a bit complex. There can be earn-out provisions and other contingency payment arrangements that depend on future earnings or some type of agreed upon benchmark, seller financing, and employment contracts for the seller that must be detailed. Even a relatively straightforward all-cash deal usually provides for some adjustments for items such as inventory, pre-paid and unpaid expenses, and similar issues.

The contract will detail the methods of payment. If it is a lump sum cash payment, the contract will state so. If it is an installment payment, the purchase agreement or an ancillary document will have to provide for the period over which the installments have to be paid, the rate of interest, the form of the promissory note, and the installment schedule, as well as the definition of the kind of security that you are pledging (if any) to the seller to guarantee the payments. If part of the purchase price is to be paid in installments, the seller will want to get as much security as possible. That is, he will likely want to hold a security interest in all the assets of the business being sold, the furniture, fixtures, receivables, inventory, and so on. He may also want to secure the installments with other assets that your company owns. It is, of course, in your interest to pledge as little security as possible. In any case, the actual security stipulations must be agreed to and reduced to writing.

Operation of the Business Between Contract and Closing

Most P&S agreements warrant that the seller has maintained the status quo of the business up until the closing as required by the LoI. That is, the owner kept prices approximately the same, kept the inventory at normal levels, maintained employment status, kept the same hours, and so on.   In the event that you had to make material changes in the business between the signing of the LoI and the closing, your lawyer should exclude those changes from the warrantee.

Non-compete Agreement (Covenant not to Compete)

In nearly all cases, when you buy a company, you should insist that a seller agree not to compete with you for a minimum period of time. Generally, non-compete agreements are for two to five years. However, be careful in preparing the non-compete agreement. For a non-compete agreement to stand up in court, it usually must be significantly limited in scope. If, for example, a seller of a regional environmental remediation firm agrees not to compete in the environmental remediation industry anywhere in the U.S. for five years, a judge would probably rule the agreement too broad and invalidate it. Note that the court would not alter the agreement, but would invalidate it completely, meaning that the seller would be free to compete with the business he sold, even to the extent of opening up right across the street.

A non-compete agreement limited in scope to the region where the environmental company is located is much more likely to be upheld by the court, and therefore is more valuable to you. However, it is usually not considered overly broad for a non-compete agreement to provide that the seller is not allowed to contact the customers of the business he sold, should the seller go into business outside the range provided in the agreement.

A non-compete agreement with a seller of a business that is truly national in scope that stipulates the whole U.S. as the geographic range would likely hold up. Many online businesses, even very small ones, can reasonably argue that they are national in scope. Therefore, a non-complete agreement with the seller of an online business that is selling nationally could specify the whole U.S. and likely stand up if it found its way to court.

Don't fall for the trick some sellers use of offering a very broad non-compete agreement that they know cannot be enforced. The rationale guiding non-compete agreements is that a person cannot be overly restricted in his right to earn a living in a free market system.

Seldom are non-compete agreements serious impediments to closing a deal.

A non-compete agreement can provide a tax advantage to you in some instances. This is covered in detail in Chapter VIII.

Warranties

For the most part, the warranties are those that the seller gives to the buyer. These typically include some or all of the following:

(1) The seller has the right or authority to sell the business that he is selling.

(2) The assets that the seller is selling are unencumbered by any liens or other such claims (see subsection above: Liens and Encumbrances).

(3) The financial information, which was provided in writing to the buyer, fairly represents the financial situation of the seller.

(4) There have been no major changes in the business since the financial documents were prepared.

(5) The leases and other contracts that are being assigned to the buyer are in full force and effect.

(6) There are no lawsuits or other litigation against the seller except those that have been disclosed, if any.

(7) Any licenses or permits that are necessary for the business are in effect.

(8) The equipment being sold is in good working order (except as specified).

(9) The inventories are at a certain level, and that any deviation from the level will be adjusted at closing.

(10) The receivables (if included in the sale) are at the stated amount, and should they vary, price will be adjusted up or down at the closing.

As the buyer, you will be asked to provide few warranties, if any.

In practice, you will probably be asked to sign a non-disclosure agreement (also called confidentiality agreement) early on in the discussion phase. This agreement may also state that you will not use any information gained to the seller's disadvantage. If you are buying a competitor you will want any NDA to be carefully drafted or reviewed by your lawyer so that it does not interfere with your ongoing operations.

A breach of warrantee may or may not be material. To simplify the process while still protecting both parties, the indemnification for breaches of warrantees and representations may be subject to a basket and cap arrangement, which is discussed later in this chapter.

Other Adjustments

Items in this category are often the most difficult and quarrelsome. Some of the items of adjustment are rather straightforward, such as utility and rent adjustments. That is, an adjustment is made for any utility bills that will have straddled the closing and therefore be incurred partly during the seller's ownership of the company, and partly during your ownership after the closing. Likewise, if rent is prepaid on the first of the month and the transaction closes on the tenth, you will owe the seller two-thirds of a month's rent, unless other arrangements are made. Other items, such as prepaid insurance and security deposits, must also be adjusted. Also, adjustments for bills received after the closing that are shared responsibility must be adjusted. Several other types of adjustments are a bit less straightforward and warrant consideration and discussion. Let's look at three examples:

Example 1.

Assume that you are acquiring a business in June and that you are planning to retain the employees. Traditionally, in this particular business, vacations are taken in July and August. Some sort of adjustment may be needed to account for the fact that the vacations have been earned for work in the previous year, but the burden of paying for these vacations will now fall on you. There can be different solutions for this problem, such as money being set aside in escrow, or paid to the employees prior to the closing. This kind of issue and others like it must be discussed and settled in writing.

Example 2.

In this example, we'll assume that you are acquiring a going business, but the receivables are not included in the sale. Customer "X" owes money for previous purchases. After the closing, he buys more goods and then sends in a partial payment. Should the payment be applied to the previous owner's receivables, to your own receivables, or should it be somehow divided? This kind of situation should be decided before closing the sale.

Example 3.

In this example, let's suppose you are buying a retail company that has a rather liberal policy of returns and exchanges. To retain the customers' goodwill, you decide to continue the liberal return policy. After the closing, several customers come in and ask to return goods. Who is going to be responsible for the refunds? Several solutions to this kind of issue are possible, but once again it all must be carefully thought out and agreed to in advance.

True Up

Neither buyer nor seller wants to be bothered with minor discrepancies that will most certainly pop up after the sale is closed. Purchase and sale agreements often stipulate various conditions where seller owes a credit to the buyer (or vice-versa). Generally, the sales agreement will be based on a net balance sheet at closing that will include A/P, A/R, inventory, work in process, etc. Once all of the bills have come in, the receivables collected, etc. the actual balance sheet at closing is compared to the net balance sheet upon which the price was based and there is a *true up*, where either the buyer pays for a higher balance sheet or is compensated for a smaller one. As in the representations and warrantees these claims may be subject to a "basket and ceiling" or "basket and cap" arrangement.

Basket and Cap

A seller wants to know once they have sold their business that unless they have committed fraud they are no longer at risk from the performance of that business. A buyer wants to know that they are not going to face significant unexpected expenses. However, nobody is interested in making very small adjustments to the purchase price after the close. Hence, many Purchase and Sale agreements contain basket and ceiling provisions.

A basket accumulates costs to the buyer associated with breaches in representations and warrantees or for which the seller should have been responsible. For example, if the buyer found post-closing that a factory required a discharge permit renewal fee paid pre-closing and paid $5,000 for it that expense would go in the basket. If a customer returns a defective item bought pre-closing the amount of the refund might be added in as well. If the basket stays below a threshold defined in the agreement nothing happens. However, if the amount in the basket exceeds that threshold, the seller is responsible for the excess costs. A tipping basket may also be created. If the basket is a tipping basket then once the costs exceed the threshold the seller is responsible for all of the expenses (from the first dollar put into the basket). So, if there are $25,100 in claims against a $25,000 basket, the seller would have to pay $100, but if the basket is a tipping basket the seller would need to $25,100.

Baskets may also have a cap or ceiling. In this case, the seller's maximum liability is also defined. Ceilings may exclude claims based on deliberate fraud. Generally, sellers will get a ceiling far lower than the purchase price of the business, though a ceiling that equals the purchase price is not unheard of. Sellers try to exclude consequential damages, damages based on lost expected earnings, and damages for which the buyer is compensated in other ways (for example by an insurance company).

In complex transactions there can be ceilings and floors on specific types of claims. For example, there might be a total basket of $50,000 for the total transaction, but a warrantee claim basket that tips at $25,000. There may be a limitation (ceiling) on all claims of $2,000,000, but an agreement to limit claims for environmental remediation to $1,000,000.

Often, claims against a basket can be offset against a seller provided note or money left in escrow so that the buyer does not need to try to collect from the seller post-close.

In addition to a basket, there may be a bucket: a place to accumulate unexpected revenues due to the seller. Let's say a payment for A/R that was previously written off is paid post-closing, a refund for an overpayment is received, etc. These can be accumulated in a bucket and only paid out if they exceed a threshold.

Attorney's Fees

Even for the purchase of a very small business, the legal expenses entailed in transacting it are substantial. It can easily cost several thousand dollars to have the agreement(s) drawn, for advice along the way, and for the actual closing. The purchase and sale agreement is a major part of the expense.

If the seller's lawyer draws that agreement, your legal bill will be lower, but it may be false economy. Many buyers feel that they will be better protected if their own lawyer writes the agreement.

Lawyers generally charge by the hour. The fact that the transaction is relatively small in dollar amount may not reduce the time needed to prepare the required documents and attend the closing proportionately with the size of the business.

Choosing an Attorney

The period between signing a letter of intent and the actual closing can be a difficult one. Lots of things have to happen. Due diligence is typically the most arduous and time-consuming activity of the LoI to closing period. The legal process, though, is a close second. There are a plethora of documents and demands going back and forth between buyer's and seller's lawyers. The process is, of course, necessary. However, it can be significantly less painful and time consuming if the lawyers on both sides are experienced in the business buy-sell process. Lawyers not familiar with the process need to spend a lot of time researching various issues and too often insist on excessive protection against eventualities that are very unlikely to happen. However, when you have two lawyers who know the process, know what needs worrying about and what doesn't, and have a pretty good sense where the legal negotiations will end up, the process will be far quicker and more efficient. We have seen lawyers unfamiliar with mergers and acquisitions kill deals that should have been consummated. We have also seen lawyers experienced in the buy/sell process be very helpful in rescuing deals that got into trouble.

If you already have an attorney with whom you are happy, who is familiar with business transfers, by all means use that attorney. However, many fine lawyers with extensive experience in general law do not have appropriate experience in this area. It is possible that your company attorney who has served you well for 20 years is not the best choice of a lawyer to assist you with buying your business.

XII. Due Diligence

Up until this phase, you have learned about the business that you are looking to acquire. The offer that you made in the letter of intent was based largely on the information that management provided to you. Now that the owners of the business that you are acquiring have agreed to sell, you have a period of due diligence, which is the time that you can verify that representations which the seller made were accurate and complete.

Items that need to be checked during due diligence include:

Financial Audit

You may want to hire a CPA to perform a thorough audit of several years of financial statements, looking for material discrepancies from the financial statements that you have received. In addition to tying to bank statements, financial statements should also be tied to tax returns. With the owners' authorization, copies of the tax returns that were filed can be obtained directly from the IRS by filing form 4506. A transcript of the return, which is not an exact copy but can be used to verify the figures on the return, can also be acquired with form 4506-T. However, it can take 60 days to receive the returns from the IRS.

A financial audit must also include an analysis of accounts receivable. Serious past due accounts can be a red flag, showing that a major customer is in trouble, exposing you to significant risk (including credit risk if you are acquiring the receivables). Even if the customer's financial situation is sound, serious past due receivables may point to a relationship that is developing troubles.

Payroll

You need to check payroll records to ensure not only that they match the financial statements, but also to verify that the figures that you used to determine the owners' compensation, and hence excess earnings, were accurate. Even in an asset sale, the IRS can hold the acquirer liable for unpaid payroll taxes, so it is vital that you ensure all of the payroll taxes have been paid.

Legal

You need to make sure that the business owns all of the assets that you are acquiring, including intellectual property such as patents, trademarks, and business names. Any real estate must be unencumbered by liens. Loans that are secured by the company's assets must be paid off at or before closing, unless you are assuming those loans as part of the deal.

As a buyer, you want to be certain that you will not acquire an unanticipated liability, especially if the deal is structured as a stock sale. It is vital that you understand all pending and threatened litigation. Finally, if you are acquiring real estate, you need to make sure that an environmental assessment is done so that you are sure that the site does not require a cleanup. A competent attorney can assist you with these issues.

Inventory

If the physical assets that you are acquiring have material value, it is important that you take a physical inventory of those assets. Inventory can include raw materials and work in process in addition to finished goods. You want to ensure that all of the inventory and other assets that you are acquiring are present and in good condition.

Employee and Customer Relations

Often, a seller is reluctant to allow the buyer to have direct contact with the employees and customers before the deal is consummated, since it is embarrassing and potentially damaging to explain why a deal fell through if the sale does not close. Therefore, the buyer may not be able to talk to key employees and customers until the due diligence period. Sometimes, talking to employees and customers is deferred until late in the process, after the buyer has agreed that the financial and other due diligence items are acceptable. Although doing so is difficult, if there are key employees or customers the loss of which would impact the value of the company, it is vitally important to make sure that they are happy with the company that you are buying.

We have sometimes come up with creative ways to allow a prospective buyer to ask questions of employees and customers without revealing why. For example, one of the authors sold his firm, which was ISO 9001 registered. As part of the quality management system employee and customer satisfaction was routinely assessed twice a year. The buyer was allowed to add questions to the questionnaire that was used for that assessment as part of the due diligence process. We have also seen buyers ask customers for a reference using a vague explanation such as "We are considering providing the company with investment capital."

Transitional Details

There are a number of small details that are often overlooked in the course of putting together a transaction. These include details such as how customer credits, gift certificates, returns, etc. are to be handled. Generally, the amounts involved are not material and we prefer to treat them like any other liability.

Another area that is often overlooked is matters related to the employees. How is accrued vacation to be handled? What does the seller do if a key employee requests vacation time for the week after the target closing date? You need to make sure that you understand how and when insurance, retirement, and other benefits will change.

XIII. After the Sale

When you buy a business, you are purchasing that company's future earnings. Unless you have purchased a distressed business, it is important to make sure that you make changes slowly and only after you thoroughly understand the business. Many of the most successful business buyers spend several months learning about the business they just bought before making major changes to it.

Your first task after a purchase is to reassure key employees that their jobs are safe. Meet with all of the employees. For transactions structured as an asset sale, you may have to formally re-hire the employees. If there are going to be any changes to pay or benefits package, you should explain those changes with appropriate sensitivity to the employees' apprehension of a change in ownership.

Ask the former owner(s) and the employees for advice and explanations. Even if you are not retaining the former owner as an employee after the closing, it is wise to try to retain him as an advisor for some period of time. Perhaps he can be retained on an as needed basis. Few sellers are unwilling to consult on an occasional basis. At the very least, we would encourage you to have him review the operations and advise you on a regular basis.

The task of transitioning the acquired company is even more difficult if you try to manage it from another location. Managing a business remotely decreases the chances that you will learn of problems with employee morale or customer dissatisfaction and will make it harder to form a bond with and inspire employees. One way to improve the odds of success if you cannot be physically present after the closing is to retain the former management team to continue running the company.

Provide recognition to the employees shortly after the sale. The recognition need not be a large bonus, even a gift certificate for dinner or a movie, delivered with a heartfelt thank you for their effort will set the tone for your relationship and help ease the employees' fears.

Once you have reassured the employees, you need to reassure key customers that the fine products and services they received will continue to be supplied without interruption. If appropriate (as in service businesses where the personnel matter a lot) you should have the former owner introduce the new owner or manager to clients. In a service business, stress that the people providing the services will not change. Let the customers know that they can contact you or the assigned manager in charge directly with any problems or concerns. In some cases, the acquisition can be relatively seamless; so seamless that customers will hardly be aware of it. For example, few customers of fuel delivery services or of boxed software providers know the owner of the company from which they are buying their oil or software.

It may be possible to operate the new business independently while still enjoying economies of scale. You may find that you are able to cross-sell to existing customers or you may be able to combine raw materials orders. Where you need to merge operations to achieve economies of scale, do so slowly, using discrete steps that do not cause a loss of key employees or customer confidence.

XIV. Common Mistakes

In most cases, when one company buys another, it works out quite well. The purchasing company already knows the industry and has done the appropriate acquisition research and planning. However, in some cases, mistakes are made. Some mistakes are minor, while others can kill a promising deal. We have assembled this list of some of the more common mistakes that we've seen made by strategic buyers. Sure, it's great to learn from your mistakes, but it's even better to learn from the mistakes of others, so that you don't make them yourself.

The Buyer's Sense of Rational Business Decision Making is the Same as Yours

The decision to sell is not just a financial or even just a logical one to many business owners. There are financial considerations, but there are also family, lifestyle, and other factors that impact the seller's thinking. As the company's owner, he has the luxury of setting his own priorities and using whatever logic he wishes.

We're not saying that your logic doesn't apply. It certainly does apply for you and your company, and it may also match the seller's logic. However, it is also possible that the seller is applying a whole different framework of analysis to the situation than you are, and his analysis may be illogical from your perspective.

Of course, you need to analyze an acquisition as to the degree it meets your own company's goals. It would certainly be a mistake to do otherwise. However, it would also be a mistake to assume that the seller is bound to using the same system of analysis that you are using.

This is Only about Money

It is said that cash is the language of business transactions. There are even popular slogans like, "When someone says it's not about money, it means it's about money." Money is an important element of a business acquisition to both buyer and seller. However, it's a mistake to assume that the amount of money is the only important consideration for a seller, or even that it is the most important consideration. While it is easy to negotiate the money, most sellers are very much concerned about other factors like their legacy and their independence.

Yes, the dollars and how they will be paid is important. However, you need to at least be sensitive to those issues that are important to a seller, though some are not the kind of things that can be negotiated in a business transaction.

We were once sitting in on a negotiation session between a potential buyer and a seller. The seller had run his business for 40 years, and had employees that had worked for him for decades—their entire adult lives. He had formed friendships with the employees and was very concerned about the future prospects for his employees and had brought up the subject several times previously. Predictably, the subject came up again in this negotiation session and the buyer said, "Why are you so concerned about your employees? They only like you because you sign their paycheck." As one of the authors tried to intercede, the potential buyer drove a final nail into this deals coffin by continuing, "My dad used to say that if one of his employee was walking past him, lying on the ground in flames, the worker wouldn't stop to pee on the flames if it weren't for the paycheck."

Trying to Impress a Seller with the Size of Your Company

Entrepreneurial sellers may be impressed by the size of your company, but not in the way you might hope. Most small business owners subscribe to a value system that respects entrepreneurial achievement more than established size and stability. Talking about how many millions of dollars your sales were last year will likely get the owners of your target company thinking about how you can surely afford to pay more for his company.

Talk more about your firm's entrepreneurial roots and how you encourage entrepreneurial thinking than about how big your company is, and, by inference, how small and insignificant his business is.

Insulting Seller Right from the Start

Chances are good that a business that you are considering for acquisition was started years ago by its current owner. Or perhaps the current owner bought it from the founder and built it up to what it is today. In either case, the prospective seller lived and breathed that business, struggled to make it work, likely putting in 70- or 80-hour weeks for at least some period of time while building it. He probably knows how to run that business very well, or at the very least believes he does.

That being the case, it's remarkable to us how often a prospective buyer will tour a business, ask the seller a few questions, and then start offering what he believes is great advice that the seller should appreciate. "Gee, what you need is an updated website," or "You should have these products manufactured in China," or other well-meaning advice that insults the seller. Why is the seller insulted? Put yourself in his position: Suppose he toured your company or your department and after 10 or 15 minutes told you how you could do your job better. You too would consider him to be, at best, somewhat presumptuous.

It's easy to unintentionally insult a prospective seller, and doing so will certainly get you off on the wrong foot. Remember, the seller is looking for a positive home for the business he built as well as a good relationship with the new owner of his company. Be respectful of the seller's sensitivities. If you have ideas as to how to improve his business, note them and save them for later use.

Not Setting Soft Barriers Early in the Process

Once you've had an initial expression of interest from a prospective seller, you need to establish a rapport. Meet with the seller, admire his operation, tell him about your company, and allow him to ask questions. Take the seller out to lunch, drinks, or dinner if that is what it takes. By this point you've probably signed a non-disclosure agreement, but reassure the seller that you will keep information he provides confidential.

Once you have established a good rapport, set a soft barrier for the seller to conquer so that you can determine if the seller is seriously interested in getting the transaction done. A soft barrier is a task that is relatively easy, but requires that the seller expend some time and effort. Often, there is information that can be relatively easily complied by the seller, and which will be very useful in determining the valuation of the company; asking for that information is a reasonable soft barrier to set. If the seller is unwilling or unable to accomplish tasks at an early stage, then the deal is unlikely to close. You are better off finding out that the seller is unable or unwilling to put the effort into closing a deal when you're 10% into the process than when you are 90% of the way there.

Buying a Business without Getting Title to Critical Assets

When eBay bought Skype, they needed software to run the service. Unfortunately for eBay, the founders of Skype retained the software and the patents on which the software was based. They then licensed the software back to eBay. This arrangement created major difficulties, including expensive lawsuits for eBay when they decided to sell Skype

If there is a crucial asset, license, or supplier, make sure that you don't pay for a business that will be hobbled by lack of access to that asset. If the asset is controlled by the seller, insist on perpetual rights.

Using Racist, Sexist, Homophobic, or Offensive Language

Imagine a business broker sitting in a meeting between two parties that are contemplating a deal and hearing one of the parties say "They always try to Jew me down," knowing full well that there are several Jewish people in the room. Imagine an older seller telling a potential buyer "Well, someone has to wear the pants in a business," when that buyer is a successful businesswoman. As business brokers we have heard it all. A single insult to an ethnic, religious, or racial group can kill hours of rapport building.

Focusing Only on the Details that You Best Understand

Most small business owners have to be generalists. Because they don't have large professional staffs, they have to be in charge of marketing, finance, operations, personnel, and all other areas of their business. Larger companies tend to have more specialization, and, of course, more specialists. There is an accounting department to deal with accounting and finance, a human resources department that handles personnel issues, a marketing department, etc. Each is run by someone who specializes in that department's functional responsibilities.

As a practical matter, a lot of smaller companies could benefit from an acquisition by a larger company that has a more developed infrastructure and more functional expertise. One frequent problem that arises is when a specialist in an area focuses his evaluation on the aspects of the target company that he best understands and doesn't give enough attention to the big picture. Accountants and finance specialists tend to concentrate on tax issues, performance ratios, and aging schedules. Marketing experts look at marketing strategies and ad budgets, while HR people look at personnel policies. All these functions are important. But more important in your analysis is how they all work together or don't work together. It's very possible that a company with an ad budget out of line as a percentage of sales and average accounts receivable collection worse than industry average is also highly profitable with great growth potential. Look at the big picture.

Setting Inflexible Terms

Buyers *and* sellers alike tend to set strict parameters right from the start. We can't count the number of times a seller has told us he will only consider an all-cash deal, or that a prospective buyer will only look at companies with EBITDA that is at least 10% of gross revenue. The problem is good opportunities are few and far between, and they don't always fit preset parameters. The stricter your upfront limitations, the less likely you are to find a doable deal.

Buying and selling a business is a complex transaction. A lot of needs have to be satisfied on both sides for a deal to make sense. This is why intermediaries need to have a whole range of tools to make an acquisition happen. If both sides can be flexible, some these tools like earn-outs, issuance of preferred stock, and many other solutions can be brought into play to bridge seemingly unbridgeable gaps.

Years ago, we nearly lost a deal because a printing company had a major piece of equipment under lease and the prospective buyer had a policy of never leasing equipment. The lessor would not let the lessee out of the three-year agreement. The seller had a predetermined minimum amount they needed at close. To make a long story short, we were able to persuade the buyer to bend his no-leasing policy in return for the seller accepting some of their purchase price in escrow instead of cash at closing. It turned out to be a win-win, once both sides agreed to relax their inflexible demands.

Valuing Based on Comparables that are not Truly Comparable

We ran a report from a prominent data provider who now offers free valuations based solely on these comparables at the request of a buyer who was purchasing non-emergency medical transportation companies. Unfortunately, the report did not help much with the valuation. Let's look at some of the issues with the report.

To begin with, although the data provider was a reasonably large player and the database contained about 17,000 transactions, no category was narrow enough to match in the specific industry in which our client was interested, so we ended up using a category titled "Services – Local Passenger Transportation." We got a result based on 34 sales over a five-year period, a period that included wide fluctuations not just in the market for small businesses, but also in things like the price of gasoline that had disproportionate impact on this industry.

The average Cash Flow Multiplier was about 2.4, the median was 1.9. Could our client conclude that a seller who was asking 1.5 times EBITDA was offering a bargain and one who was asking for 3 times EBITDA was asking top dollar? Not really. If we look at the descriptions and limit ourselves to transactions that had occurred within the last year, we find only two transactions are left, not enough to base any real conclusions on. Their multiples of cash flow were 2.47X and 3.64X.

What is more important than what we know about these companies is what we don't know. In this report, we had no idea how strong the balance sheets of each company were and medical transportation is a capital-intensive business. Even if we had the balance sheet, there are many things that can affect the numbers on that balance sheet making two balance sheets hard to compare without an in-depth analysis. For example, choosing a different method of depreciation can materially affect the value of the balance sheet.

There are also things that are never reflected on a financial statement. A business in a rural area will sell for less than one near a major city. A business that is growing is more attractive than one that is not. Unless you know a lot about the businesses being compared, you can't decide how relevant the information is.

Most business comparable reports don't contain enough data to allow a reasonable assessment of true value. It's like trying to assign a value to a house based only on the square footage, the number of bedrooms, the number of bathrooms, and the fact that it is in Los Angeles. To get real value you would need to know what shape the house was in, what neighborhood, etc. Anybody who tries to value a home on the basis of broad averages would not be taken seriously. Unfortunately, businesses that are even harder to value fairly based on comparables are sometimes valued in just that way.

Waiting Too Long to Issue a Non-Binding Proposal

There are very good reasons to avoid making an offer or any type of binding proposal prematurely. That's why we advocate a preliminary step: the non-binding proposal. It doesn't serve either party well to spend a good deal of time and resources only to learn that they are so far apart that a deal is just not a reasonable possibility. A non-binding proposal, or a term sheet, is merely a document that the buyer issues to outline his thinking in somewhat general terms to establish whether the two sides are in deal making range. If the seller's minimum is maybe 10% or even 20% above the buyer's range, a deal may happen. However, if the seller insists on at least double the buyer's range, it's best to find this out early in the process to avoid meetings and discussions that are likely heading nowhere.

The non-binding proposal is discussed in Chapter VIII.

Trying to Do Due Diligence Early in the Process

Verifying that all you've been told is true and nothing has been left out is an absolutely essential step in buying a business. However, the verification step is properly carried out after buyer and seller have agreed on a deal, at least in principle. We advise buyers to initially assume (within reason) that all they've been told is true and to make an initial non-binding proposal on that basis. Of course, any document presented to the buyer, including the non-binding ones, should state, "Subject to due diligence verification."

Sellers are understandably suspicious of requests for detailed information before price and terms have at least been discussed, if not fully settled. As noted above, it serves all parties well if buyer and seller are within deal making range before spending a lot of time and money.

Once price and other terms have been worked out, the due diligence period begins and should be carried out thoroughly and carefully.

Overly Complex Proposals or Offers

As we've said throughout, buying a business is a complex transaction. However, that complexity should be minimized at the beginning. In a large business, something as important as an offer to purchase the company, even a non-binding offer, would go immediately to the legal department. Smaller companies, of course, have no legal departments and prefer to keep outside legal expenses down. A proposal that is in plain English with easy-to-understand basic terms will receive a better reception from a seller than will a complex one in legal language.

We've seen a number of instances where a seller looks at a long and complicated Letter of Intent, and after a few minutes says something like, "This is too complicated. I'll have to run it by my lawyer and I'm not even sure it's worth it." Of course this kind of situation only happens when the buyer has ignored our advice to keep the initial LoI or proposal simple.

After the Sale

Once the closing is completed, you have a new company to run and to integrate into your enterprise. This book deals with the lead up to this point more than with running your new company. However, there are two mistakes we have seen so often that we have to include them here.

Changing Too Much Too Soon

Chances are you have lots of good plans for improving the business you just bought. However, our advice is to go slow. Most professional business buyers spend a few months observing operations of their new acquisition to learn what works and what doesn't. Only after they have a thorough understanding do they make major changes. This restraint is not only good policy in that you'll better understand what needs adjustment, but it is also better in that current employees will be reassured by the normalcy following the ownership transition.

Under Utilizing Existing Management

You may believe that you can run your new company better than existing management has been running it, and you may be right. This may have even been one of the reasons you bought the company. However, before essentially demoting current management, it is important to learn why they do things the way they do. There may be very good reasons for certain policies and practices that aren't obvious from initial observation. Also, there are internal and external relationships that have been important to the company and will be invaluable to you during the somewhat fragile transition to your ownership.

Before you go...

Did you enjoy this book? Did you find useful information about growing your company by acquisition? We would very much appreciate it if take a moment to write a review on Amazon.

If for some reason you are not happy with our book, please contact us using the contact information on the next page and we will personally refund your purchase price.

Thank you!

David Annis & Gary Schine

Contact the Authors

Gary Schine

gary@mergers-acquisitoins.com

401 751 3320

David Annis

david@mergers-acquisitions.com

517 878 5014

ABOUT THE AUTHORS

David Annis

David has worked in fields as diverse as molecular cardiology, information technology management, software and website development, and legal administration. During his career he acted as principal in both the acquisition and sale of businesses. After selling his software company in 2003, he joined Merfeld & Schine, Inc. specializing in identifying strategic acquisitions for private equity groups. He holds an MBA from the University of Michigan and a BS from Cornell University.

Gary Schine

Gary has been a mergers & acquisitions intermediary and consultant since 1990. He has arranged and successfully consummated over 100 transactions on behalf of his clients. Gary is the author of several books on the subject including *How To Sell Your Business For More Money* and *How You Can Buy a Business Without Overpaying* (co-author).   He holds an MBA degree from the University of Connecticut.

Made in the USA
Columbia, SC
21 August 2022

65775230R00128